PRAISE FOR MICHELLE T. J
Guide to Redefining Their

"Black Out: A Black Perso
Outside of Corporate Ame
rate-based comfort zone int
passion. Read it, heed it and learn the benefits of living your dream and
sharing your passion, power and perseverance."

> —Terrie Williams, Founder, The Stay Strong Foundation / Founder,
> The Terrie Williams Agency / National Bestselling Author
> *The Personal Touch: What You really Need to Succeed in Today's*
> *Fast-Paced Business World*
> *Stay Strong: Simple Life Lessons for Teens*
> *A Plentiful Harvest: Creating Balance and Harmony Through the*
> *Seven Living Virtues*
> *Black Pain: It Just Looks Like We're Not Hurting*

"Few books say it better or simpler than this one. **Black Out** is an uncom-
plicated overview on how to live a rewarding career and life. I was
inspired by Michelle T. Johnson's insight, wisdom and willingness to
share the important lessons she has learned along her path to success.
This book is a must read for all those who are serious about avoiding the
pitfalls of corporate life or climbing one's own ladder of success. My hat
goes off to Michelle for such an important contribution to our
community."

> —**George C. Fraser**
> **Author,** *Success Runs In Our Race*

"Many self-made millionaires have realized their dreams by overcoming
odds that seemed insuperable. You have to be certain that you have the
necessary tolerance for risk if you choose to tread the path of an entrepreneur. **MICHELLE T. JOHNSON challenges you to leave the confines of**
your corporate job and tread a career path that has no limits."

> —**Melvin B. Miller, Publisher/Editor, The Bay State Banner**
> **Author,** *How to Get Rich When You Ain't Got Nothing*

"It is not that we don't have the power, it is that we do not hold the power. It slips through our fingers at the rate of 500 Billion dollars per year. In *BLACK OUT*, you are challenged to take a good look at yourself, measure your strengths and **determine if your passion is worth pursuing to gain you the power you have dreamt about.**"

—Dorothy Pitman Hughes

Author, *Wake Up and Smell the Dollars! Whose Inner City is This Anyway!*

"*BLACK OUT* is **provocative, insightful and real!** Michelle T. Johnson has scratched the itch of inspiration!"

—Paula McCoy-Pinderhughes

Author, *How to Be an Entrepreneur and Keep Your Sanity – The African American Handbook & Guide to Owning, Building and Maintaining Successfully Your own Business*

"*BLACK OUT* is a must read for African-Americans who feel trapped in corporate America. Michelle T. Johnson **offers a blueprint for those who want to strike out on their own.**"

—John V. Elmore

Author, *Fighting for Your Life: The African American Criminal Justice Survival Guide*

Partner, Harter, Secrest & Emery, LLP

BLACK OUT:

The Black Person's Guide to Redefining
A Career Path
Outside of Corporate America

BLACK OUT:

The Black Person's Guide to Redefining
A Career Path
Outside of Corporate America

Michelle T. Johnson

Amber Books
Phoenix
New York   Los Angeles

BLACK OUT: The Black Person's Guide to Redefining A Career Path
Outside of Corporate America

By Michelle T. Johnson
Published by:
Amber Books
A Division of Amber Communications Group, Inc.
1334 East Chandler Boulevard, Suite 5-D67
Phoenix, AZ 85048
Amberbk@aol.com
WWW.AMBERBOOKS.COM

Tony Rose, Publisher/Editorial Director Samuel P. Peabody, Associate Publisher
Yvonne Rose, Associate Publisher/Senior Editor The Printed Page, Book Design
Pittershawn Palmer, Editor

© Copyright 2006 by Michelle T. Johnson
ISBN#: 978-0-9767735-9-7
Library of Congress Control Number: 200693422

Dedication

This book is dedicated to all the black travelers who believe in the Power given them to create their destinies and build new worlds for generations who follow with their passion and joy.

Dedication

Acknowledgments

Recently, I finally learned the difference between the planting terms "perennials" and "annuals." I don't garden and had always gotten the terms mixed up; mistakenly thinking that it was the annuals that just come up every year no matter what you did. It turns out I was wrong. It is the perennials that take root and provide beauty, growth and stability year after year, usually able to survive natural as well as manmade disasters.

So, for this book, I'd like to acknowledge my perennials—my mother and grandmother, Ethel M. Johnson and Cliffie M. Owens, my two sisters of the heart Adrienne Bennett and LaSandra Pearl Morrison and my dogs, Hilbert and Henry.

While there are many people to thank, I wanted to both thank and acknowledge the perennials for providing love, support and roots that reach the center of the earth.

Contents

Foreword

Passion is one of the most intense emotions one can experience. In *Black Out: The Black Person's Guide to Redefining A Career Path Outside of Corporate America*, Michelle T. Johnson encourages you to step out of the corporate box, release your safety net, and experience the power of passion. When you give in to your passion, the rewards can be extensive. Passion triggers a strong sense of fulfillment and invigorates us to gain power.

The power is in every one of us to do anything we want. What separates the men from the boys, the women from the girls, those who make it and those who don't, the ordinary and the extraordinary, is perseverance. There are no excuses for not being able to do what you want to do. Sure there are obstacles—I know obstacles. I found out about obstacles, after finishing college and grad school and taking a job that was a natural extension of my training and education. I believe we are supposed to turn obstacles into stepping-stones.

I had learned that I was on the wrong path. With all those years— and all that tuition—under the bridge, with an undergraduate degree in psychology and sociology and a master's of science degree in social work, I realized that this was not the profession I really wanted. So, like Michelle T. Johnson, I decided to move beyond "survival" and take a leap of faith in search of my passion.

On February 1, 1988 I started my own company by signing two of the biggest names in the world, even before I officially opened the doors: Eddie Murphy and Miles Davis. The legal documents and the incorporation papers had been signed, and The Terrie Williams Agency, a full-service public relations, marketing, and communications firm, officially began doing business.

Our list of clients steadily grew, and within the first year we also represented Anita Baker, Jackie Joyner-Kersee and Essence Communications. Over the years, The Terrie Williams Agency diversified into all areas of public relations and marketing, with a roster of the foremost entertainers, sports stars, film companies, business corporations, publishing houses, authors and political figures. The word had spread about our services and we became known as "the most powerful Black-owned public relations firm in the country, representing hundreds of well-known entities, including: Bobby Brown, Janet Jackson, Martin Lawrence, Russell Simmons, Dave Winfield, Warrington & Reginald Hudlin, The Disney Channel, HBO, Miramax Films, AT&T, The Coca Cola Bottling Company of New York, Simon & Schuster...the list goes on.

When I began, I had no agency experience and no money. What I did have was a unique formula for success combined with a distinctive work ethic—involving attention to detail, drive, determination, honesty and integrity—with a way of life that revolved around the fact that we are all human beings.

I had never formally studied public relations, marketing or communications; but after earning my master's I worked at New York Hospital for about two years, using my education. The demands of the job made me frustrated and depressed; and to make matters worse I was not at all happy about my limited salary.

After about two years on the job, I realized that things had to change and I knew it was time to take a risk. As fate would have it, I met and befriended Miles Davis who was a patient at the hospital and he impacted my destiny. My education and experience had focused on dealing with people; but by now I knew that the hospital and social work did not fit into my plan for fulfillment.

As I became more curious about the entertainment industry, my avenues of opportunity began to open wider. I networked, interned, freelanced, studied and networked some more; and with a new lease on life, I reached back to use the principles of achievement that my parents had instilled in me as a child. I had been taught the importance of finding a way to do what I wanted and needed to do.

All of us are born with a need for passion…but not all of us are fortunate enough to understand what that passion is. Survival is a part of our instinct…we expect it. We may be fortunate enough to survive for many years, but without passion, we will never experience true joy. This book can guide you beyond your corporate-based comfort zone into an exciting new career empowered by your passion. Read it, heed it and learn the benefits of living your dream and sharing your passion, power and perseverance. Stay Strong and remember to share your light.

—Terrie M. Williams, Author,
Founder, The Stay Strong Foundation
The Personal Touch: What You Really Need to
Succeed in Today's
Fast-Paced Business World
Stay Strong: Simple Life Lessons for Teens
A Plentiful Harvest: Creating Balance and
Harmony Through the Seven Living Virtues
Black Pain: It Just Looks Like We're Not Hurting

Introduction

Life loves to be taken by the lapel and told:
I'm with you kid. Let's go.
—Maya Angelou

Cruising Out of Corporate America in Search of Passion

People need hope. People need passion. When you're dealing with survival issues, that's when you need hope. When you've mastered survival issues, you crave passion. In other words, you start focusing not just on what you need, but what you want, in some cases, what your soul screams for.

There are times in life, sometimes few and far between, when you leap out of bed thinking about the joy of what's coming next. You experience the untarnished excitement of being like a kid who looks forward to the day at the amusement park or their birthday party or all the wrapped gifts under the Christmas tree.

Hope. Passion. Joy. Excitement. Those are invigorating words. They make you skip the snooze button and head straight for the new day.

Then there is survival. Survival makes you crawl out of bed.

Survival is worrying about getting a job when you don't have one or holding on to the job you've got. Or survival is about getting more money to make ends meet as the ends move further and further apart. When you can't stand your boss, that's survival. When you're convinced your boss can't stand you, that's survival. When you feel discrimination nipping at your heels, that's survival. When you can't see your job as anything more than the time between showing up and quitting, that is survival with a capital S.

Getting past survival to the point where we can feel relative contentment is a level a great number of black employees manage to reach. According to the Bureau of Labor Statistics the unemployment rate for blacks still remains double the unemployment rate for whites, yet many blacks manage to keep their heads above water. The mortgage or rent gets paid. The car note gets sent to the financing company every month. We're able to clothe and feed our kids as well as ourselves. Some of us even manage to get a few brand names charged to a plump line of credit. If nothing else, the ends meet.

But as someone who has been in survival mode as well as the mode where the ends meet quite nicely, I've learned the hard way that I'd rather drink from the cup of passion than sip on a cracked glass of hope.

And what I've found frequently with others is that while people seek water when they're thirsty, they bask in the sunlight when they've been well fed.

When You're Interested in More Than Just Survival

My book *Working While Black: The Black Person's Guide to Success in the White Workplace* was about survival in the workplace. In fact, I describe the categories of black employees as being survivors, strivers or thrivers and aspiring to be drivers. However, at its most basic level, the thrust of the book *Working While Black* was about entering an environment created before you got there (the world of

Corporate America) and learning how to negotiate it on your terms, how to survive.

Although the point of *Working While Black* wasn't to be negative, it's hard to write about such a daunting subject and not feel an occasional heaviness. Work is heady stuff. Regardless of what color you are or what you aspire to do, the subject of work is about those basic needs, the ones that people don't get all warm and fuzzy over.

Working While Black, really was a book meant to be proactive and empowering yet realistic. However, I'll be the first to admit that the topic was akin to giving decorating advice to prisoners on how to spruce up a jail cell. Not all black workers view themselves as serving a term in Corporate America prison. At the very least, some of the years worked in "traditional" jobs does end up feeling like a term we're serving.

While traveling the country in early 2004 to promote *Working While Black*, I was saddened by the consistent despair I encountered from blacks in the workplace. Whether from high level executives speaking in hushed whispers so as not to be overheard by white colleagues, or younger blacks already stung by crass workplace dynamics even before getting their first degree—the pain and fatigue were thick enough to touch.

Throughout the year, I got a stream of emails from black workers who expressed appreciation that someone had straightforwardly addressed their issues without sugar coating the facts.

At the tail end of the book tour when I started mentioning this book, it was amazing to see the excitement this topic generated. A book about how to leave Corporate America? A book about blacks who already left Corporate America and are happy and not living in a cardboard box over a heating grate? A book about people who pursue their dreams and actually make them real? A book directed to blacks that doesn't have as its underlying premise that we should be grateful to have a job?

I found that people could support a book about creating a fulfilling and passionate life. Because the truth of the matter is, if you had the time and money to come to a book signing you probably weren't dealing with baseline survival issues. Bills generally were getting paid even if it wasn't the best use of your money to buy a book. The kids and pets were sleeping indoors. Your boss actually smiled at you most days.

But, like many Americans, regardless of race or background, playing it safe can begin to feel like living in a velvet cage with a diamond door handle, where the surroundings look really good but you're still stuck in a cage. In the back of our minds we always ponder, what happens outside the cage. Is it really that rough out there?

Some of us who have disposable income still managed to hang on to some of those wild and wacky dreams. Most of us might be fat, but we weren't full.

People wanted to know: what about the passion, what about the joy?

I knew I was on to a great topic when I sent an e-mail around looking for people to interview. Relying on only the names of the people in my computer address book, I sought out blacks who made their living avoiding or leaving Corporate America.

Within days, I got responses from people all over the country who left Corporate America or who avoided Corporate America in the first place to start their own publications, to be an engineer by day and model and actress by night, to write romances and mysteries, to start consulting companies, and dozens of other exciting, off the beaten track career paths.

Some of these people were enthusiastic about wanting to be included in my book but hard to track down once I had actual questions. I didn't take it personally. That was because as someone creating a new path for myself with no blueprint to work from, I know that it can be hard to get to things that don't contribute directly and immediately to the bottom line. For me, it was just gratifying to know that I was on the right track writing this book.

I personally understood well the need for passion. In fact, I've had friends accurately comment that my books on blacks in the workplace were mimicking my life. My first book was to advise blacks on how to survive and succeed in the predominantly white workplace as a black person and then this follow up book is how to leave Corporate America and create your own path.

It's not so much that my life went from riches to rags; it's just that I developed a new appreciation for the assorted uses of rags and the infinite variety of riches. Moving from being a black attorney in a society that puts far too much weight on having a legal degree to being a poor, almost bankrupt writer and consultant has allowed me to build a different life for myself based on nothing short of passion.

I got to the point where I couldn't practice law any longer. I felt like I was wearing a gray, itchy suit with a choke collar. I felt it, the law firm I worked for felt it, the people in my life who loved me felt it. And the only direction to move in, was out.

Truth was, as much as I loved to write, I hated writing legal motions and legal documents in general and wasn't very good at it. It's almost funny now to admit that .

I wrote *Working While Black* while working as a black attorney and living in the state of $90,000 a year if not quite the county. By the time the book came out I was regularly dipping into my 401-K savings trying to live as a full-time writer. That didn't work well financially, so I got a part-time consulting job as a human-resources director and employment consultant to help pay the bills.

I felt I was no longer a member of the Corporate America rank and file. I defined myself as a writer, I had people actually paying me occasionally for what I wrote and I never had to think about billable hours and legal motions again.

Granted, it hasn't been easy seeing my savings trickle away. And it pinched my pride to accept that I could no longer single-handedly handle the mortgage or upkeep of a house every month.

But being a writer, and having an actual writing career fills my heart with joy. I glow when people tell me they've read what I've written and find it helpful and insightful. I'm at peace when I make the time in a day to focus on my writing.

For me, leaving Corporate America to pursue my passion changed everything in my life for the good. I had to say goodbye to people, places and things that no longer suited my path. The people, places and things that remained were embraced with a new appreciation. Don't get me wrong, letting go of who and what no longer supported me was not easy. There were days when it was extremely painful. But once I started on my path, there truly was no turning back. And the people who stayed with me, trial after tribulation, got to share the benefits with me. They were the people who loved me for my core and not for the outer shield of conventional armor.

I once said to a friend that finding passion in life was like a log bobbing down a river. When a log is in the river, everything has to flow around the log. That solid mass isn't dissolving to accommodate anything else. Sometimes the log moves firmly and serenely down the river at its own pace. Sometimes, it rushes quickly, pushing everything smaller and less sturdy out of its way. But the log remains what it is and anything smaller and flimsier has to make its way around the log or reach an impasse where the log and the lesser debris get stuck together.

When your passion is a log in the river of your life—anything that lacks the log's sturdiness and weight just has to adjust or move out of the way.

So, this book is about figuring out how to make your passion central to your livelihood—how to build that log.

Why the Issue of Leaving Corporate America is Different for Blacks

If you find passion in Corporate America, power to you. There are people, including blacks Americans, who have secure, lucrative lives to show for it.

But more blacks making more money does not necessarily equate to more blacks being happy.

And that's what the point of this book is about. If your path is that of traditional 9 to 5 but you don't view your W-2 forms as a love letter to employment, then figure out the exact route of your particular path and follow it. Follow it so that other blacks will see your joy and have a role model for creating greater happiness.

One of the things that inspired me to write this book was that I noticed many of the books written about the dissatisfaction in Corporate America and the pursuit of doing something different, more creative with your life seemed to be directed to only one group– white America.

One particular author got great publicity and bestseller status for his book because he focused on how to figure out how to restructure your career path to find greater meaning. Good book. Great message. But based on the pictures of the people in the book, the book's target audience primarily appealed to one group in this society- the white middle class and those who identified with the white middle class.

Don't get me wrong—my implication is not that he was being racist. He wrote to the target audience of which he was a member. As with many of the other people who write books like this, most of them are not deliberately trying to exclude people of color.

The idea of work being anything other than a way to pay for your life is a luxury. Having a job that you like, let alone love, isn't just a bonus, it is perceived by many to be a luxury. And let's face it; black society is not usually encouraged to think this is a luxury that extends to us. Hell, if we used the beginning of time as our starting point, metaphorically, getting paid for work in America, as opposed to being forced to do so as part of your slave labor, was a luxury we just got yesterday. But, to the extent that working for personal satisfaction is a luxury, it still seems to apply to that narrow margin of us—those who have the talent to be athletes or entertainers or who are fortunate enough to take over the family business or who hear the voice of God and seek out the ministry.

But to truly move forward in our society, I think blacks can't afford to think of creating our own opportunities as nothing more than a luxury for white folks.

You see, we live in a society where people either like to go to one extreme of dismissing or marginalizing the legitimate issues of black people or the other extreme of completely drenching us in the issue of race.

This book is targeted to black employees. Although others can read it, it's directed at blacks because so many of the other books written about work as a creative force are not directed at us.

Almost every time I've spoken on the book *Working While Black* there is a white person in the audience who points out that many of the issues discussed aren't just "black" issues. Maybe not, but the perspective is. And when you fail to see examples that represent you, you begin to think that maybe the examples don't apply.

For example, we know that when the white CEO quits his six-figure job to open a bakery, it is not about the person's race. But on a gut level many blacks will not see that as our reality because culturally we are conditioned to believe that more opportunities exist for whites and that more negative consequences exist for blacks who might pursue the same, unconventional path.

And that's not just speculation or "chip on the shoulder" racial whining—statistics on employment, on average weekly income, on loan approval, on many other things that affect making a big career decision—bear that out. Therefore, when our foundation seems more rickety to start with, it can be harder to realistically give thought to adding a new deck onto the existing structure. Worse yet, it's harder to think about tearing down the existing structure to build another.

Bottom line, it's about how you think of the renovation projection before you even pick up a hammer. In other words, it's often more about the psychological impediments than the tangible ones.

I know, for example, that my worry in pursuing the writing life comes from having a loving family that silently, and not so silently, have questioned why I would want to leave the guaranteed security of practicing law for the poor, more erratic life of writing. Sure, many white families have frowned with disapproval at their artsy loved ones, but with black families we know it was a chore to get through the doors of Corporate America in the first place. So why leave?

I, on the other hand, believe the opposite. If you're unhappy, why stay?

In 1943, the behaviorist Abraham Maslow came up with a theory of human motivation that argued that people operate from a hierarchy of needs. Under this theory, you don't find yourself being able to move to the next level of need until the lower, more immediate needs, are satisfied. The most basic need is physiological, then safety, love, esteem and self-actualization.

According to Maslow, the need for food is at your most basic level —physiological. Your body is crying out to be fed and you can't think past that. If you need a job to pay for the food then your need is safety. When the basic needs are satisfied then you usually are driven by the need to love and be loved, which are considered social needs. After those needs are met then you can be motivated for more, such as working on your confidence and sense of achievement to create and enhance your self-esteem. And only after these needs are met do you have a need for self-actualization, which is the need for happiness, the ultimate luxury.

As a cultural reality, many black Americans, even the successful ones, find it a long climb to get to those higher needs of Maslow's scale.

I'd venture to say that even when some of us make tons of money and have fancy homes and cars to match we still operate in a scarcity mentality because the fall to poverty doesn't seem very far away. Scarcity mentality is a spiritual principle based on how you see the world affects the world you see, therefore if you deep down believe you're not supposed to have much or that you're destined to be poor, then even if you win a $2 million lottery, scarcity mentality will make you feel as if it is still not enough. And for many black people that mentality can be reinforced by what we see around us since, even the most well off blacks can remember a family member having to dip into the welfare system or live in neighborhoods you won't see in the guide books.

For example, the highest black justice on the Supreme Court, Clarence Thomas, dogged his sister for being on welfare for about all of five minutes back in the 1970s. Though not a psychologist, I'd argue that Justice Thomas suffers from a little bit of that black scarcity mentality himself where having a sibling on the system hits a little too close to home, making him want to put as much distance as he can between where his life is and where his life could be as a black man in America.

You Do Have the Choice to Creatively Create Your Own Livelihood

If this book does anything, I hope that it opens minds to the possibility that we are not indulging in an extravagant notion to consider building an unconventional career path away from the hallowed halls of Corporate America. I'm not trying to suggest there needs to be a mass exodus. But I do want Black Americans to entertain the same power of choice that is encouraged (or at least not routinely disparaged) in the households of the majority.

My viewpoint is that happiness is not a luxury or an indulgence. I won't even say it's a basic. I think happiness is a decision. And I believe the decision to be happy while deciding how we are going to spend key waking hours that add up to significant years of our lives should be viewed as your birthright.

Chapter One

When Strivers and Thrivers Become Travelers"

How far you go in life depends on your being tender with the young,
compassionate with the aged, sympathetic with the striving,
and tolerant of the weak and strong.
Because some day in life you will have been all these.
—George Washington Carver

Signpost: What are the internal and external factors that contribute to black employees reconsidering whether traditional Corporate America is the place for them. And what defines Corporate America anyway?

Why Do Some Blacks Decide to Leave Corporate America Once They've Entered It

My previous book was titled *Working While Black: The Black Person's Guide to Success in the White Workplace.* While the title wasn't my creation, it ended up being a very accurate, bold title for the book I did end up writing—a book on navigating and negotiating the halls of Corporate America as a black person.

The reason this book is directed at just blacks is because I wanted to write a book that spoke to our desire to expect more from this life than just forty acres and a mule. (Or, for these modern times, forty acres and a paycheck.)

My experience came not only from working since the age of 14 but from being an employment attorney during most of the eight years I practiced law.

As a black person who was also an attorney, the twist was that most of my years as an employment attorney were spent representing corporations in their lawsuits brought against them by employees.

Representing employers against litigation and EEOC claims ranging from race to age to gender to other unlawful reasons listed by the law gave me a unique perspective on how employers think. For one, as hard as it is for most employees to believe, particularly minority employees, most companies are not headed by card-carrying bigots. In fact, many of the people at the head of the organizations are genuinely shocked when they get sued for discrimination because they assumed that everyone beneath them reasons fairly when making employment decisions.

Sure, there are cases where the employers are deliberately and pointedly encouraging systemic discrimination; but those cases make the newspapers because they are the exception, not the rule.

Having said that, the innate ignorance that people operate under is a different story. And if you're the victim of someone else's ignorance it sometimes doesn't matter whether you're being screwed willfully and intentionally or screwed accidentally based on ignorance. Also, in your mind, the distinction between whether it's your co-worker or your immediate supervisor or the company CEO making your life a walking hell doesn't matter.

So, no matter how much I came to understand the legitimate expectations and standards of well meaning, honest employers, I also instinctively understood that for black people in the workplace, we operate from our own unique situation in the pecking order.

When I met people all over the country who had read *Working While Black*, I was gratified to see that what I wrote resonated with the black audiences. I have only found myself talking once with a predominantly white audience about the book and needless to say there were a lot of blank looks, not hostile but blank. On reflection I begin to better understand the great divide between how blacks and whites view the situation with blacks in America—blacks feel our experience, whites often times merely intellectualize it and thus struggle with understanding our collective anger.

Facts and Perceptions Regarding Black America

Among the reasons why blacks and whites have different perceptions of the workplace and thus, why this book is directed specifically at blacks is the following:

- White men are twice as likely to get management jobs over equally qualified black men; and three times as likely as black women. (Ryan A. Smith & James Elliot, "Race, Gender and Workplace Power," *American Sociological Review*, June 2004.)

- In 2001, the average financial wealth for black households was approximately 12% of the average for all white households. ("Minorities," in State of Working America 2004-2005, *Economic Policy Institute*)

- According to a July 2004 Gallup poll, while 77% of whites believe that blacks have equal job opportunities, just 41% of blacks believe they have the same job opportunities as whites.

- In 2003 Northwestern University sociologist Devah Pager, studied the treatment of job applicants in Milwaukee, Wisconsin to focus on the likelihood of a job applicant being called back based on whether they had a criminal record with comparable resumes sent to the same set of employers.

One of the most poignant numbers from the study were that only 14 percent of blacks with*out* a criminal record were called back for an interview compared to 17 percent of whites *with* a criminal record.

- A Gallup poll from January 2004 shows that blacks in America do not achieve the same level of personal contentment in our society as whites with only 37 percent saying they were "very satisfied" with their lives as whole, compared to 55 percent of whites who expressed that level of contentment. Job dissatisfaction was listed as one of the reasons why blacks had lower numbers.

- Also, when black employees and others use the legal system to achieve equity in the workplace, compared to other people who file lawsuits, those with employment discrimination cases have fewer cases settled before trial, win fewer cases, and face more appeals and reversals. (Kevin M. Clermont and Stewart J. Schwab, *How Employment Discrimination Plaintiffs Fare in Federal Court*, Cornell Law School, July 2004)

Black Employees In Corporate America

These facts and findings demonstrate that black Americans are forced to work in Corporate America with numerous issues gnawing at their heels as they attempt to climb the ladder of success.

Even the findings about discrimination lawsuits illustrate that regardless of the basis for discrimination, justice can offer cold comfort if you try to prove you're not getting a fair shake.

In writing *Working While Black*, based on both personal and professional experiences, I knew that there was not a one-size-fits-all mentality that applied to all blacks in the workforce.

My observation is that there are roughly three types of blacks who were in Corporate America. Yes, I know that individualism makes each of us unique. I know that each of us is an amazing blend of experience, personality, upbringing, genetics and dozens, if not thousands of other nuances that make us special.

But when it comes to the knee jerk, default mentality that governs how a black person handles the workplace, I've observed that there are three general kinds of archetypes that determine whether you're the type to make the leap out of Corporate America.

I call these employees survivors, strivers and thrivers. I believe we're all a little of each and that circumstances will dictate a change in our style.

A survivor is the type of black employee who goes to work, does the job, doesn't think much beyond the politics of collecting a pay-check and tries to draw little if any attention to himself if possible. You know the survivor in the workplace because you basically don't know her. The survivor is too busy focusing on the daily necessities of getting the job done to be a well known commodity.

A striver is the type of black employee who is particularly ambitious and thus primarily focused on striving to get ahead. Ambition—that's the mantra of a striver. A little attention doesn't bother a striver as long as it's the kind that generates them the kind of perks they crave. And a lot of attention doesn't bother a striver if it allows them to skip up several rungs on the ladder of personal ambition and success.

A thriver is not necessarily thriving in the workplace but they do thrive in their own spirit. A thriver has no desire to accommodate their individual style to the workplace. If they come off as "ghetto" in a backdrop of stuffy, blue suits, that's who they are. If they're a little India Arie in a department full of Gwyneth Paltrow wannabees, thrive on. If their taste runs more to a basketball game in the neighborhood in a corporation that believes weekly golf games are good business, yep, that's a thriver.

In the workplace, black survivors, strivers and thrivers can, as individuals, create great work experiences. When a black person works in a fair, well run, balanced workplace that appreciates diversity and recognizes good work across the board then it often times doesn't much matter whether a black is a survivor, striver or thriver. I've always said a functional and fair workplace is a thing of unparalleled beauty.

But the truth is most blacks don't find the workplace to be the fair, above board setting it should be. In addition to ordinary politics that plague everyone regardless of color, almost all black employees eventually find themselves engaging in a game of pin-the-tail-on-the-Negro, where many black employees feel that their behavior in the workplace is disproportionately scrutinized and then when a problem is discovered harsher penalties levied. That may sound like a negative concept but unfortunately it turns out to be a realistic one.

Someone recently asked me if I had discovered anything surprising while visiting various cities to talk about my book. I said, actually, I was hoping to be surprised. I was hoping that the blacks in their 20s just starting in the workplace would have different stories than the blacks in their 60s facing the twilight years of their careers when it came to black issues. The stories weren't different. And that makes me sad.

I think that the blacks most likely to feel the disconnect between what society says the workplace should be and what the actual experience turns out to be are those blacks who are extraordinarily ambitious (strivers) and extraordinarily individualistic in style (thrivers).

You see, some black employees, like those across all racial and ethnic lines don't find intrinsic value in being an employee. It's strictly arithmetic for them. If I work X hours at Y rate then I make Z dollars. That's it. That's all the workplace exists for. I don't go there for friends, for fame, for acclaim, for validation. The Gwen Guthrie song "Ain't Nothing Going On But the Rent" would be that kind of employee's theme song.

Now, because more internal motivation takes place with the ambitious strivers and individual thrivers in how they view the workplace, they are the ones likely to give more thought to making their way out of a structured workplace.

A striver (a black employee driven by ambition) finds that her light shines more brightly when her ambition is fed. A striver looks to the workplace to validate his need for recognition in what he does. External validation of internal ambition rings a striver's bell.

A thriver (a black employee driven by the need for individualism) puts the light on his own personal style. Whether a waitress or a CEO, a black thriver concerns herself more with being able to do a job her way. A black thriver is his own man who doesn't want to compromise who that is no matter how uncomfortable that makes anyone else in the workplace feel.

In the first season of the NBC television show "The Apprentice," Donald Trump had a bunch of people running around in circles competing for the honor of running one of his companies. The two blacks on that show were good examples of the difference between one who is motivated by ambition like a striver or motivated by exerting their individual style like a thriver.

Kwame, the smooth Harvard educated brother with the laid back style, was the prototype for a black striver. He wore his ambition well, clearly wanting the job but being very measured about how he handled himself with Trump and the other competitors as he kept his eye on the ball.

Omarosa, on the other hand, was perceived as a very negative incarnation of a thriver. She let her style, her personality, her imprint overpower her performance on the job. Granted, Omarosa was far more over-the-top than the average thriver. But you get the idea. The well channeled power of a thriver can get an employee ahead in the right situation. However, if not properly handled it will leave people with a bad taste in their mouth.

Since strivers and thrivers (those fueled by ambition and individualism) seek more than just security and a paycheck, they are the ones much more likely to seek their particular passions outside of traditional Corporate America.

What Exactly Is Corporate America?

That leads me to defining what I mean by Corporate America. People tend to think of it as a literal concept involving only big corporations.

But Corporate America for me is more of a philosophy than a concrete kind of place. Yes, Corporate America does mean the big corporations—the ones that appear on the Fortune 500 list. And the ones that appear on the Fortune 5,000 list. It also includes government, little companies, even small businesses where you're a cog in someone else's lucrative machine.

Corporate America also includes those high status jobs that people get overly impressed with, but who the person holding down the job thinks of as just a job. Those include jobs like being a lawyer or doctor or engineer, even being a teacher. People love the idea of a person having those kinds of titles.

Basically, if acquiring your pay or salary comes fueled by someone else's agenda, you're working for Corporate America.

When you like working in Corporate America, or at least don't mind it, it's like the fence around a piece of property or a glass that holds water. The rules and boundaries don't bother you. Even working hard to make someone else rich doesn't bother you. But when you're not feeling Corporate America and it's not feeling you, it's the noose around your neck, it's the shackles gripping your ankles. When working in the confines of Corporate America keeps you up at night or makes you not want to get out of bed in the morning, it starts feeling like an institution with bars and padded cells.

Just like there is no value judgment attached to whether one is a survivor, striver or thriver in the workplace, especially since they are my own personal designations, I don't think Corporate America is an inherently evil place. Therefore, at least for me, there is no value judgment attached to the black employees who actually prefer working in it.

Some do think that Corporate America is the devil's playground. I have a friend, who isn't black, who does think of Corporate America that way and views her departure from it to raise her children akin to completing a prison sentence.

However, while I departed from traditional Corporate America after 17 full-time years (including the "break" to go to law school), I know that it has as many benefits as it does pitfalls. There is something to be said for the structure and the security and the organization that Corporate America can offer the life of an employee.

As a member of society, I appreciate that dedicated employees work at all the places that make my life easier—people who work in all levels of government, people who work in the utility companies, hospitals, restaurants, retail businesses were I shop, and emergency personnel. Without employers to hire employees there might be chaos in this country. When you live in any part of the country where there is ice and snow, you have great appreciation for the legion of employees who salt the streets.

As of the beginning of 2005, approximately 148.1 million Americans are in the work force and counting, according to the Department of Labor.

Given that, I'm aware that many people work in jobs that are not a good fit for their souls. What's worse, however, is when you've carefully selected a profession or a career and still don't find that fit. By that I mean the people who have gotten tons of education and acquired experience in an area of expertise only to one day decide that's just not how they want to live their work lives anymore.

One thing to make clear in this book is that I recognize that not every black person is dissatisfied with Corporate America and their fit in it. I also recognize that people change their view on where they want their careers to be. Someone can be perfectly content in their 20s and 30s or even their 40s and 50s and like a dormant bud bursting into a flower, decide Corporate America no longer fits.

For those people or for those times in your life when Corporate America works for you, then you can find your job enjoyable and pleasant and maybe even develop an emotional attachment to it.

But when you know in your heart that Corporate America or your particular role in Corporate America no longer is the spot for you then you don't feel passion or joy or even strong emotional attachment. At best you feel disconnect, at worst you feel down right resentment.

And if it's a position that you have by way of a lot of education, training or some other climb up the corporate ladder then it can turn into a job that you're supposed to love but that you don't, even though every one, including yourself, thinks you should.

A very good friend of mine who received a professional degree almost a dozen years ago has gone through more than a dozen jobs in the space of that time because she kept trying to force herself to fit into a box she created. She kept trying to love those jobs and develop an emotional attachment to them.

It wasn't until she defied convention and expectation and got a low-status, medium-pay "temp" job to pay her bills that she found real freedom. Freedom to go back to school, freedom to leave a profession she hated but felt she had committed to and freedom to work at a job just for the money so she could pursue her passion to work with children as a counselor.

Like my friend, it was when I got the prestigious legal jobs that I was supposed to love—when I got my "real" jobs that came attached with position and prestige that I ultimately became miserable. At some point I accepted that I'm just not a good employee. While I can deal with rules, regulations and guidelines I agree with, I don't like doing things other people's way for no other reason than because they are higher on the corporate food chain than I am.

The big "aha" moment I had was when I made the connection that the essence of being an employee is keeping track of knowing your place on the ladder and adhering to the general concept that you always answer to the people higher up on the ladder. Always. Not when you feel like it. Not when you like the boss. Not when you agree with the boss, but always.

Where I've been fortunate (or smarter some would say) is that the professional jobs I obtained allowed for a certain degree of independence. As a newspaper reporter and then later as an attorney I could sometimes operate under the illusion that I was higher on the workplace pecking order than I really was. But the bottom line was that I was always a small cog in a much larger machine.

While working recently in a consulting job as the on-site human resources director for a predominantly black and medium-sized business, I learned that I was far from being the only person who had a problem with the existence of hierarchy. I'd say that a good 75% of the employee problems I dealt with involved people having an even bigger problem with hierarchy in the workplace than I did.

What Tends To Push Or Lure Blacks Out of Corporate America?

Which leads to what this book is about. At some point when the ambitious and the fiercely independent decide to leave Corporate America they become something else.

The "something else" is the strivers and thrivers who become travelers—someone who moves away from the traditional, expected way of doing things. A traveler is a black person who decides to create their own path out of traditional Corporate America.

Just like it's a type of mindset, a default mechanism, whether you're a striver or thriver in the workplace (one who operates primarily motivated by ambition or individualism), it's the same mechanism that determines whether you become a traveler.

What triggers the transition from workplace contentment to hitting the road and becoming a traveler? The reasons are as individual and diverse as the people, but I think the reasons fall into three general categories.

1. They're hating life. More specifically they're hating their work life. A boss or a whole group of bosses or a company leadership philosophy drives them nuts. Or the environment you work in irritates you to your last working nerve. Ultimately, you just dread going to work or feel that it routinely saps your spirit.

2. Work feels more like a bad fit. When this is the issue, you know that on the surface nothing is wrong with your workplace. You get along well with the people. You don't hate your job or your career. You can actually even be considered very good at your job by the powers that be. It just no longer rings your chimes.

3. You get slapped in the face by some grand cosmic event. You get laid off or fired from your job and fate forces you to create an opportunity for yourself. Basically, you're not making a choice

but you actually feel good about the outcome once the ground beneath you begins to feel firmer.

While all of these reasons can infect an employee, regardless of race, these reasons can be particularly pernicious as a black person because it seems as if fewer role models exist for blacks in figuring out how to find a way out of the corporate rat race.

Whether you run from what you hate, rise from what no longer serves you or deal with life out of necessity, you become a black person who travels out of the workplace to create your destiny.

Famous black travelers include the following: John H. Johnson who started a publishing empire that included *Ebony* and *Jet* Magazines from using his mother's furniture as collateral for a $500 loan, Al Jarreau with a degree and career as a rehabilitation counselor who goes on to become one of the most well known jazz singers of his generation, and Pamela Thomas-Graham, a sistah who runs cable news channel CNBC while writing bestselling mysteries in her "spare" time.

The next chapter discusses the different paths of the traveler.

- A black traveler is an employee who decides that after pursuing the course of ambition or individualism in traditional Corporate America, that way is no longer for them and they seek a way out.

- Corporate America, as defined in this book, is a place of employment governed by a set of rules and expectations that allows little room for individual self-expression to get the job done.

Traveling out of Corporate America is about pursing a path that works for you and helps you create a life and pursue a livelihood based on passion and joy.

Chapter Two

What is a Traveler and What Does the Map Look Like?

If there is a better solution. . . .find it.
—Thomas Edison

Signpost: What are the alternatives for creating a way to make a living out of traditional Corporate America? They typically include, starting your own business, pursuing art, being an independent contractor or trading in status for an unusual career. What are some questions to ask yourself about your journey out of Corporate America? Is it copping out or opting out?

What Does The Path Away From Corporate America Look Like?

I believe it's all about the journey. When I was an employee, I was an employee who started out with a head full of ambition (a striver) and eventually became a person much more concerned about imprinting my personal style on the workplace (a thriver).

To me, there just has to be meaning surrounding how you will make a living. While my life has been less stressful in some ways when I worked for the money and more secure finances, my happiness has always come when I found my motivation in something larger than the job itself.

Most travelers become motivated by the journey, by the meaning beyond the employee handbook.

At some point in her life, Stephanie Renee was well on the road of traditional Corporate America. She was a student at the prestigious Wharton school getting her degree in marketing and legal studies and the future looked not just bright but safe.

But at some point, her love for art and her distain for traditional conformity called her name and she answered back. Now, Stephanie Renee owns two companies, including Creators Child Productions and Queen Bee Creator. She is also a performing artist.

"Being a Wharton student gives you a comprehensive insider's perspective on what Corporate America is capable of and might expect from its employees," Renee says. "I knew that I could never flourish in an environment that generally expects high levels of conformity and suppression of one's cultural self. By the time I got to senior year in college, I was busy trying to figure out how to put my education to use without doing any of what my family and my professors had been grooming me toward. That's a scary place."

Renee was fortunate in that she got the light bulb inspiration earlier rather than later. She figured out first, rather than by trial and error, while she was still in school and still able to make far-reaching adjustments. While one can always make a change, unquestionably it's easier to do so when you're at the beginning of a major phase of your life rather than in the middle of one you've already invested a lot of sweat equity in to.

Because the journey away from or outside of Corporate America is a journey that makes sense to your soul, that makes you glow. There's only a handful of ways it tends to be done by blacks although there is an infinite variety within those paths.

Blacks deal differently with the realities of the world and our realities are significant and actual. Such as: (1) The reality is that in good times or in bad, whether under the regime of a Republican or Democratic president, blacks typically have double the rate of unemployment of whites; (2) The fact is that according to the EEOC, 35% of the discrimination complaints in 2003 were based on race; (3) The facts, according to the U.S. Census Bureau in 2003, is that blacks who earn a college degree are no more likely to get a job than whites who drop out; that the same holds true for black high school graduates versus white high school dropouts and that regardless of the degree held—Bachelor's, Master's or Doctorate, Blacks earn less than their white counterparts.

There are far more facts I could write about concerning the discrepancies and disparities faced and perceived by blacks in Corporate America but the point is that the differences form the invisible dividing line that complicates the work experience for black Americans.

Emotional "Realities" Cause Many Blacks To Look Outside of Traditional Employment

In addition to the realities that blacks face in the workplace, emotional "realities" can dodge every step also.

The emotional realities include knowing in your gut that you have to work harder than your white counterparts, that you have much less margin of error than your white co-workers when you err and that discipline, whether fairly deserved or not, will often times be swifter and harsher than those of your white peers.

Black employees quickly learn that the moment they express either an emotion regarding treatment or a perceived reality about the workplace that doesn't correspond with the boss' then the phrases "troublemaker," "chip on their shoulder," "playing the race card" or some other career-damaging characterization will be slapped on to them to minimize, if not eradicate, their perspective. Even if a white person is more well meaning and doesn't go that far, they will quickly dismiss the soundness of any such viewpoint because they don't want to believe you're correct or they resent that a chance exists that you may be.

Regardless of the motivation, your actual and perceived realities are often met with phrases such as, "that's ridiculous" or "you're wrong" or "you can't prove that." The irony is that the people who are the quickest to dismiss a perspective that is founded on you being black are often the first to rely on their own perspective to explain something negative that happened to them. It amazes me how many white males I've heard say that they can't get a break anymore because of affirmative action and diversity initiatives or white females who dismiss the possibility of racial animus in a spe- cific situation while simultaneously bemoaning the legitimate gender discrimination they endure.

All of this is to say that the general experience of being black in the workplace is one that breeds a struggle to hold on for dear life. It's not always a sinking ship but it can often feel like a rocky boat with limited life preservers to pass around.

I have this general theory, probably shared by many, that the reason the typical disgruntled employee who goes in with a gun and blasts away co-workers is usually a white man is because that is the one group in our society (if not disabled, gay or otherwise marginalized) raised to believe that things are supposed to go their way because of their inherent merit.

In fact, the Workplace Violence Research Institute lists among the common traits of perpetrators of workplace violence, white male, between ages of 35 and 45, does not take criticism well, chronically disgruntled and almost always places blame externally. (Addition- ally, usually has a preoccupation with guns and firearms, which explains the distinction between saying that most white men in the workplace commit violence and most who commit workplace violence are white men.)

When you believe that doing the right things, saying the right things, having the right looks and acquiring the right habits equals success, and you live a life where others appear to be looking and living just like you, the world can look like an oyster with you feeling like a pearl. You even start to believe that when bad things happen to others, it is because they failed to do the "right" thing. Therefore, if some bad outcome finds its way to you, of course it's unfair and unjustified. Combined with a precarious mental state, it's a good combination for grabbing a gun and trying to dish out some old-fashioned justice.

When it comes to feeling that life can just be inherently unfair, the life of the average black man or woman is so different. There's not a black man or woman alive in their right mind who won't tell you that they learned at an early age that their racial makeup will be noted. Depending on a lot of things, the lessons may be bitter, thoughtful, angry, hurtful, or helpful. Regardless, the lessons learned mean that the bad stuff at work will often cause you to flinch but not crumble.

Therefore, while blacks might be a lot less likely, according to statistics, to turn their pain and anger outward by way of shooting up workplaces, the pain and the anger doesn't evaporate. Those negative emotions oftentimes manifest in poor health, poor relationships, and destructive behavior—or just a slow, insidious deadening of the spirit.

Worse than that, the actual statistics and anecdotal evidence we observe in our lives leaves us feeling like we're saddled with limited options and limited healthy outlets.

But hope exists. There are travelers on the path out of Corporate America who have transformed fear and bitterness and just plain unfamiliarity into a life that works for them.

Walking Out the Door Rather Than Running Out the Door of Corporate America

This book is about the black travelers who create paths that don't lead them to the door of power structures created by other people. Some never start there in the first place. And others start in Corporate America but leave it with a plan. It might be a fuzzy, haphazard plan held together with bubblegum and spit, but it's a plan nonetheless.

I say that because merely walking out the door of your job with an "I'm outta here" and a few choice curse words doesn't constitute building a career plan of passion. Sure, you may have passionately loved telling your now former boss where he or she can shove it, (I know I sure did many, many years and two careers ago when I was much younger) but that's operating from a reactionary standpoint that doesn't really get you anything other than a good story to tell.

Being reactionary may help contribute to the timing but it can rarely be a substitute for a plan itself.

Let me provide an example. Your boss has given you the blues for years. One day, you walk into his office and he tells you that you're not going to get the promotion you want because your commissions have been low the past few months. You leave the office angry because you know the commissions have been low because your boss has been more attached to giving the good leads to the perky young blond thing hired six months ago.

Your anger over the lack of receiving the promotion, combined with your low simmering disgust for your boss, prompts you to compose a resignation letter giving two weeks notice.

Reactionary or part of a humble plan?

For a black employee primarily motivated by raw ambition (a striver), who has always wanted to start your own business and has saved money, a seven-page business plan to be dusted off and a family situation that will only be moderately impacted by a drop in income, it is as good a plan as any.

For a black employee primarily motivated by individualism (a thriver), who has given no thought to a concrete future, has a blighted credit history, a low checking account balance and several hungry mouths to feed with every dime of your income, you didn't make a plan, you reacted.

Sure, there are gradations between reacting to an event you don't like and planning for a future you desire, but sometimes it's the distinction between enjoying the ocean waves and drowning.

Studies haven shown that one of the key tools in learning how to better handle stress is changing how you perceive a situation. In other words, it's how we view an event that determines whether it's positive or negative. Or, contrary to the saying of what you see is what you get, it's actually, what you get is what you see.

For example, getting fired from a job may on the surface be an undeniably negative event with no positive spin to put on it. But for someone who absolutely hates his job, gets a huge severance from his employer, has a wife who draws a significant salary from her own career and who had planned to quit at some point anyway, it might be the most positive thing that ever happened.

Because the flip of that would be sitting still, and feeling afraid to quit on his own and make a change. Or quitting at a less convenient time without getting the generous severance package that your particular employer offers. Or becoming so miserable you end up creating a lousy marriage and losing the loving support of the spouse with the second household paycheck.

On the other hand, a seemingly positive event in your life could be riddled with unseen disadvantages. For example, a promotion with a huge raise, more impressive title and great perks couldn't be anything other than a positive event, right? Not to a woman who has just decided she and her husband are going to try to have their first baby and who has made the decision to cut back on her hours and intensity at work in preparation for the new family, not to mention the necessary maternity leave she would need.

For that woman, she will be hitting the wall that separates her personal commitment to her family from the expectation of Corporate America that insists that you take all promotions offered. And for her, having to make that choice makes the promotion a negative event.

See? It's all about perspective. Where you stand, where you sit. Most importantly which pair of glasses you wear when you view the situation.

When you make a decision to leave Corporate America out of anger or frustration, it may appear as if you're seeing clearly. Actually, all you're doing is feeling very clearly and mistaking emotion for truth.

Four General Paths Away From Corporate America

The blacks who choose to leave Corporate America usually take one of four general paths out the door.

1. **The Path of the Emperor**—choosing to start your own business and be your own boss

2. **The Path of the Artisan**—the black employee who leaves Corporate America to pursue an artistic career

3. **The Path of the Hermit**—the black employee who decides to be a freelance member of the workforce and work as an independent contractor

4. **The Path of the Magician**—the black employee who departs from status to pursue something unconventional from typical Corporate America.

The following chapters outline the considerations and issues that a black traveler must consider when contemplating avoiding or walking away from Corporate America.

Author M. LaVora Perry knows first hand what it is like to be a black traveler in Corporate America—knowing that it wasn't so much that the corporate world was intrinsically bad, it just wasn't part of her big picture.

"Once my boss said something like this to me, 'LaVora, when most people come into a work environment and see what its rules are, they adjust to meet them. But instead of doing that, you try to make the rules adjust to fit you.' I thought, "Yeah, and what's wrong with that?"

After a time, while managing Corporate America nicely, the point came when Perry decided to create her own path with its own set of rules and become a writer of children's books.

Keep in mind, the road to being a traveler out of Corporate America is not a linear one. As I address in a later chapter, some people don't want to completely leave a traditional and conventional life, they just want to supplement their chosen life with their passionate choices.

Some people, who take that route of going part-time or spare time in their passions, often find that they can not serve two masters indefinitely. That will especially be the case the more you become engaged by the happiness that comes from pursuing what you love.

I look at my hero Gordon Parks. He has done it all and has done so fighting more barriers in a couple of years of his life than many of us will have to fight in an entire lifetime. In part, it's because he didn't make the easy choices for a black man born in Kansas in 1912. Eventually, Parks obtained the ultimate Corporate America job—he became a photographer for *Life* Magazine. Only in his case, he was the first black to hold down that job. So, he had the dual challenge of being black in his Corporate America world and being the first and thus, the only.

He then later went on to take on the ultimate Corporate America player—the federal government. He became the first black to work for the Office of War Information and the Farm Security Administration. Talk about security and a nice pension to look forward to.

But for anyone who knows the history of Gordon Parks, that's not what he did. He wasn't content to just hold tight to the "good jobs" although he remained a photographer at *Life* for 20 years. He proceeded to write 12 books, compose music, including film scores, paint, pen and direct movies including the original *Shaft*.

Parks, who died in 2006, reigns as an example of someone who reached the top of this game in a respectable and prestigious Corporate America job but still kept inventing new ways to excel and find fulfillment.

Granted, Parks did not have your typical boring, low paying job—his Corporate America job allowed him to travel the world and live a life that many affluent whites would envy. But he was still working for someone else, and during a time when a legally segregated society had no shame to its game.

But Parks still reigns as an example of a black traveler who could be successful, even acclaimed in Corporate America, but still found that to honor the leanings of his soul, he needed to step out and create his own path—in Park's case, create a whole new map.

When Is It Opting Out of Corporate America, When Is it Copping Out?

There's a fine line between escaping Corporate America and leaving it to pursue something that brings you joy.

I consider it a fine line because the distinction is a choice I don't believe the majority of blacks were raised to consider.

When it comes to pursuing the Path of the Emperor, there are pockets in black society that have always raised children to consider entrepreneurship.

In 1939, for example, nearly 30,000 blacks owned retail and restaurants generating $71 million in sales, according to the Coalition of Black Investors.

Cities where there have historically been a large concentration of blacks, such as cities and towns in the South and northern cities like Detroit and New York City, have typically had a large number of black business owners.

In my city of Kansas City, Missouri, George W. Gates and his son Ollie started a barbeque empire in 1946 that has passed down through the family, creating one of the most recognizable brand names in the city and national recognition for the bottled sauce. The children of these black barbeque barons know first hand what it is like to be born into an entrepreneurial gene pool and thus have the choices that go with that legacy.

However, owning or running a family business that you have no real passion for doesn't necessarily serve your higher purpose or feed your soul any more than operating as a nameless, faceless cog in Corporate America. Sure, you don't deal with the direct issue of race as an employee. But that's about the only perk you get if you're not passionately engrossed doing something you want to do.

Copping Out Is When You Give It No Thought, You Just Want Out

How do I define copping out? It's a judgment call but I say it's walking away from something without purpose or plan and with no real sense of why you're leaving in the first place.

I also would say that copping out, as opposed to opting out, happens when you give no thought to the effect of your actions.

If you work on an automotive assembly line, and one day the overall dissatisfaction of what you're doing overwhelms you to the point where you walk off in the middle of a shift, you may be copping out. If you leave giving no thought to the co-workers who have to work much harder to make up for your sudden departure, or without thought to how you're going to pay your mortgage or feed your eight-month-old baby, you're copping out.

In our society, it has become a growing phenomenon for young blacks from disenfranchised neighborhoods to just avoid regular employment altogether because of not wanting to be "dissed" by whites or by the general racism of white society. Instead, they hustle to pull together a living. Although their families and the educational system may have failed them to a certain extent, many of them are still copping out.

Every person shouldn't strive to attain an office job or a six-figure salary. But if you've given no thought to why you don't want to work in Corporate America and haven't thought about what you do want to do, it's a form of copping out.

Unfortunately, we tend to only recognize copping out when it's an affirmative act. Sometimes the slow, insidious drift through life, without any side rails to at least partially reign us in, can be a form of copping out if in your heart you know you want more.

Opting Out Is Having A Plan and Purpose
Opting out, on the other hand, is moving with purpose. It's moving with a conscious, purposeful resolve to depart from a situation that no longer works for you.

The same feelings exist whether you're copping out or opting out from Corporate American-dissatisfaction, hopelessness, depression, anger, fear, despair. What makes the difference is how you choose to move out of that quagmire.

Being a traveler as a black person out of Corporate America—opting out rather than copping out—is about both the destination and the journey. When you're copping out, it's just about running away with no thought to whether your feet are on gravel littered with broken glass or on a smooth, sparkly, yellow brick road.

What Are The Ways to Figure Out Whether You're Copping Out or Opting Out?

Question one—Ask yourself how you define yourself. How you feel about that definition is key.

Do you identify yourself by what you do for a living and do you feel pride, joy or anything positive about it? If a surge of negative emotions wells up in you when you say what you do, then your decision to leave Corporate America may be based on copping out.

Only you know whether the negativity has so overrun your ability to think about your workplace or career without your blood pressure going up that all you can see is getting out, not merely forward. On the other hand, if your situation has gotten that bad—where your health has you about ready to stroke out from all the tension—leaving quickly to save your life is not copping out.

Question two—Can you separate where you work from what you do?

Even though workers exercise much more job and career mobility these days, there are still a great number of people who stay with employers long enough to get to the point where they have developed either complete boredom with their jobs or have outright come to hate it.

For blacks in particular who have been brought up to crave stability, we can particularly get caught up in staying in a job so long we develop hatred for a place, in part, because we think there is no place else to go.

For example, black employees disproportionately work in government jobs compared to our overall number in the workforce. In fact, an April 2002 report by the United States Office of Personnel Management states that the federal government has hired a far higher percentage of minorities relative to their actual numbers in the civilian workforce.

Government work offers a nice, safe job. No disrespect to the millions of blacks who do work and have had employment in government, but government jobs for the most part are not deliberate choices to express inner passion.

My point is not that all government work is grey and lifeless. My mother has worked for the federal government dangerously close to 40 years because she has found ways to grow and prosper as she climbed the corporate ladder. In each job she found a way to enjoy and master her skills and it has served her well.

But many people don't thrive in those environments. And many of those people are fine without having passion for their job. Or, like my mother, they find a way to make their safe, secure jobs satisfy their souls as well.

But when you make a religion out of hating your job, maybe you should change jobs to see if it is the job itself or what you're getting from it.

Question three—With unlimited funds and total support from everyone who matters to you, what would you do?

If all you can think of are the possessions you would buy or all the debts you would pay off, maybe staying in Corporate America provides a good fit for you.

However, if you can think of experiences you want to create that also pay you money, then maybe you've tapped into your passion and you need to figure out how to make that a reality.

A close friend of mine has the desire and passion to open her own bed and breakfast hotel in a comfy, scenic country place. The reality of being an executive in a top corporation in her city is a long and far cry from following that dream.

Because she is young, she has the best of both worlds. She can save money and gather more momentum for her ultimate dream when the time and opportunity are right. But she is intuitively savvy enough to know, however, that the longer she waits the harder it will be to walk away from the security a good salary and a nice office provide.

This example serves to illustrate that there is no "right" time to make a decision. She does not have a burning desire to leave the comfort of her Corporate America job today, in part, because she likes her current job very much. However, in five years, the bed and breakfast goal may disappear from her consciousness all together as other priorities crowd that particular one out.

This book has as its focus the black employees who choose to make the move out of or away from Corporate America today rather than as goal they plan to reach.

Question four—Do you know the difference between a dream and a passion-fueled goal?

Deep in our hearts if we sit still and listen, we know the difference between a dream and a goal we would fulfill if the circumstances were right and the resources came through.

Performer Cecilia Aderonke listened to her heart. She knew that staying in her Midwestern city to teach in the local school system wasn't something that moved her. After much meditating on what was the right path for her and where she needed to be to pursue it, she decided she wanted to become an actress and a musician and she moved to New York City.

"I did a lot of internal, spiritual work to decide," Aderonke said. "I [decided] I wanted to live life creatively, where freedom was the most important thing."

Aderonke did the hard work of tip-toeing on pavement to reach as far for her star as possible. She decided to pull it from the sky and make her dream a reality—in other words, a passion-fueled goal.

A dream is one of those things we come up with when we think of the lottery numbers we may hit one day. Many people never concretely move toward dreams, they just passively acknowledge them every now and then when they're reminded.

But goals fueled by passion- the kind travelers have—involve actions over time. Sometimes actions so small they wouldn't show up under a microscope. But the small measures to make the fuzzy clear add up. It might be a library book you check out on starting your own business or a community course you take in painting or a phone call you later make to someone you meet at a party who seems to be doing exactly what you want to do.

While some might say that dreams and passions are interchangeable—since often times, one dreams about what they are passionate about—I think of them as two very distinct things when talking about creating a career or following an internal calling. Because while dreams can take you high when it comes to what you want to do, it's passion that has the ability to actually take you forward.

It doesn't matter about the time frame because sometimes it takes years for you to manifest a goal, especially if you don't have support for making these changes at a quicker pace.

And sometimes you have to try, fail, try again, fail and just keep tweaking your life as you make the dream come true. As a Buddhist saying says, an arrow hitting the bulls' eye of the target is the result of a thousand misses.

That leads to the next and last question about whether you're copping out or opting out.

Question five—Have you truly given thought to how your life and the lives of the people you are intimate with will change once you pursue your path?

When you're copping out you don't think of anything but getting out. All you can think of are the people who you will never have to speak to again, the job duties you hate that will become history; basically all the things you'll be happily letting go of.

When you're opting out you give real thought to the ways your life will change, to the sacrifices you have to make to travel out of Corporate America and make your life work. You think not just about the positive improvements but the real commitments and responsibilities that will change.

Working in Corporate America is traditional. Going to a place of business, to a government office, to an easily identifiable job is something that people hold on to harder than we realize. Even when we don't think we make the money we should for the work we do, most of us have a lot of attachment to that regular, dependable paycheck. Almost as important, most of us have a lot of attachment to the identity that comes from bringing home that paycheck. We Americans, regardless of race or color, are extremely identity driven.

So when you opt out as a traveler you probably have stopped to think of all that you are about to get yourself into. Even if you can't anticipate every roadblock, you've thought about the general cracks in the sidewalk that exist.

For example, most career changes from the traditional to the non-traditional involve a change in income and initially it's almost always less money. If it's just yourself that you have to think about with no dependent children or a spouse or other financial obligations to consider, it may not be as big a leap, but a leap it is. And if you have any person in your life who does depend on your income, that doesn't mean that you should necessarily put your goals on a shelf. That just means you have more pieces of your life to take into consideration.

Thinking Things Through Is A Form of Action

You may be asking where all this thinking gets you anyway? Isn't thinking just a waste of time, a way of avoiding real action? Not if you approach thinking as a synonym for planning.

Thinking gets you to the other side of making a decision versus merely having a reaction. We come from a long line of "doers". We were marching on Washington and learning how to withstand riots and violence directed at us at a time when large pockets of the rest of the country were learning the pleasures of meditation, "finding themselves" and "free love".

But sometimes giving a lot of thought to a life change is exactly what you need to do before you make decisions that lead you to greater action.

And only you know when that thought has crossed the line from genuine contemplation and planning to plain old procrastination.

A very powerful quote by Johann Wolfgang von Goethe says, "Each indecision brings its own delays and days are lost lamenting over lost days ... What you can do or think you can do, begin. For boldness has magic, power and genius in it."

The power is not just in making a decision, any decision, it's in having the boldness to take the first step toward it.

When you decide, no matter how flimsy the plan, you're being a traveler who uses a map to get you where you want to go. When you react, it's like driving around aimlessly without even enjoying the scenery and finding yourself stuck in the middle of someplace you definitely didn't want to be.

One of my favorite books is *Parable of the Talents* by black science fiction writer Octavia Butler. The book draws its title from a parable in the Bible that, in a nutshell, talks about how Jesus gave a varying number of talents to several servants. After a time, to the servants who used the talents they had been given, Jesus gave them more talents. To the servant who buried his one talent, he took the talent away and gave it to another servant who was actually using the talents he had already had. As Butler herself said when being interviewed about the book, the parable is a harsh lesson but a good one. It's the Biblical version of "use it or lose it."

I personally view the parable as a challenge to us mortals to assume that if we have a dream, better yet if we have a passion, if we have a desire to do something different with our lives, it's there for a reason and our Higher Power expects us to follow up on it.

The following chapters give you an idea of how to design your own path as a traveler out of Corporate America.

I repeat what I said earlier—seeking out a professional path that makes your heart sing should not be considered a luxury for any of us.

In summary:

- The four general paths out of Corporate America that this book explores are: **The Path of the Emperor** for the black employee who chooses to start their own business, **The Path of the Artisan** for the black employee who leaves Corporate America to pursue an artistic career, **The Path of the Hermit** for the black employee who decides to be a freelance member of the workforce and work as an independent contractor and **The Path of the Magician** for the black employee who decides to depart from their status job to pursue something unconventional from typical Corporate America.

- Figuring out whether your copping out of Corporate America (running away from what you hate) is different from figuring out whether you are opting out of Corporate America (creating the path you love). The bottom line is whether you're planned your exit for a larger purpose or are reacting to external negative events without giving much thought.

Chapter Three

The Path of the Emperor

Mix a conviction with a man and something happens.
—Adam Clayton Powell

Signpost: Following the Path of the Emperor is the route for black travelers who want the power and responsibility of owning their own business. This chapter describes the path and pitfalls of someone who takes on entrepreneurship, and offers the opportunity to explore if this is the path for you.

Blacks Have A Rich History of Starting Their Own Businesses

The beauty of the 21st century is that in almost every major city in America and many of the smaller ones, you can find a black business owner to take care of all your major life needs.

With persistence and a good set of contacts, you can find a black doctor, black lawyer, black dentist, black pharmacist, black insurance agent, black banker, black retail owners, black car dealer, black real estate agents and of course, a black funeral director. From cradle to grave, if you work real hard to do so, you can have most, if not all, your life needs met by black entrepreneurs.

Statistics bear that out. According to the United States Department of Commerce there are more than 3 million black-owned businesses in existence with even more growth predicted.

In February 2005, based on census data, the Secretary of Commerce stated that minority-owned businesses were growing at more than six times the national rate, with minorities owning 15 percent of the nation's businesses, employing 4.5 million people and generating almost $600 billion in gross receipts.

Therefore, of all the paths that black travelers take out of Corporate America, while scary, the path of the Emperor seems the safest and most familiar.

I call it the path of the Emperor because it's more than about being the boss. It's about being the boss' boss. It's about being super king. It's about being head queen. Ruler of the world you govern. An Emperor straight up is running things and someone who follows the path of the Emperor is not looking to rule by committee.

Deciding whether this is the path for you is similar to deciding whether you're copping out or opting out of life in Corporate America as I discussed in an earlier chapter.

What Kind of Emperor Are You?

There are basically two types of Emperors when it comes to leaving Corporate America. One type who follows the path of the Emperor is the type who wants to own her own business no matter what, and without any real concern about what kind of business she runs. She just knows she has to be the boss—period.

For example, that is the reason the real estate business appeals to some people. There are probably very few children who grew up and said, "I really want to sell four bedroom houses in needy suburban communities or condominiums in upscale downtown neighborhoods when I grow up. Maybe if I'm real lucky, I'll sell commercial real estate to urban developers!"

No offense to real estate agents, but I doubt if a lot of that is happening. However, I think that many people seeking to find a business they can grow, develop and prosper in get interested in the business because they feel they're getting to own their very own piece of the rock. It's a profession that allows you to put your name on an agency, give you an identity that is as respected as working in Corporate America and potentially make a good living.

In addition to being the boss and owner, some blacks who follow the path of the Emperor also like the idea of being a leader, of having loyal subjects to follow their directions.

Ultimately, that becomes the most important quality in being an Emperor, having a sense of leadership.

When you work in Corporate America, no matter how high you are on the ladder, there's always someone higher than you. Even if you're the CEO, there's almost always a board of directors to report to. You can be fired, replaced, demoted, downsized, outsourced, stripped of key duties, but the company will go on.

However, as the Emperor who owns your own business, you don't just run the ship, you are the ship. You have to make sure that everyone below you is doing exactly what they are supposed to be doing whether you are by yourself, you have one employee, ten employees or 100.

Part of leadership means that you have to be willing to perform all duties in your business and pay everyone else first if there is danger of not enough money to go around.

That's where leadership in your own business differs from leadership in someone else's business. Leadership in of your own business means that you have to be the first to sacrifice, sometimes the only to sacrifice. If you're the type who doesn't believe in cutting back or going without on some things, even temporarily, the leadership exhibited by those taking the path of the Emperor isn't for you.

Gary Johnson (no relation to the author) is a Management Consultant and Facilitator who lives in the Washington, D. C. area. He is also the founder and publisher of the website www.BlackMenInAmerica.com. In his previous working lives, Johnson has been an intelligence analyst, an investigator and a management trainer for the federal government.

"I took the path of hard knocks early on and then learned that I had a higher success rate when I created my own opportunities by successfully networking, being a student of the game and taking the advice of my mentors," said Johnson.

"One of the obstacles that I encounter is the ability to compete on a level playing field with other consulting companies. Sometimes being black and male is good for business, while other times, it's not so good," Johnson said.

Another quality that black Emperors must have is a higher than normal sense of organization. You have to be the kind of person who knows what needs to be done and figures out how it gets done.

Some people pride themselves on delegating well but even delegating requires a good organizer to decide what you need to hold, fold or farm out to others.

"Before I became self-employed, I spent 18 years working for the Federal government. I had a 9-5 grind, and on some days I worked from 8—to faint," Johnson says, describing his relationship with Corporate America. "[Now] I'm helping people help themselves so they can make a greater contribution to their organizations and their lives."

Another quality that goes hand in hand with both leadership and organization is being a good researcher.

Even someone who starts a business in an area they think they thoroughly know about has to do their research. Just because you did the job for years in Corporate America does not necessarily mean you know how to do the job as a self-sustaining entity.

For example, say you do maintenance work of some kind for a large utility company and decide to open your own tree cutting service. You figure that because you've cut every kind of tree in every neighborhood of the county where you live why not make money having your own business?

It's true, you may very well have the substantive knowledge to start this business. But have you thought about licensing, insurance, taxes, marketing, equipment, employees, financing? Have you even thought about tools? And I don't just mean the physical tools, although that can be expensive and extensive. I mean have you thought about the people who can help you tool a business—an accountant, a lawyer, a tax preparer, a marketing expert? In other words, have you thought about not just doing the job but running the business?

Looking Good While Doing It Well

As a black person who decided to be an Emperor, you have to give particular thought to looking like your business acumen is tight, right and pulled together.

Any person who has ever started a new business will be the first to tell you that the details you don't take care of or that you handle sloppily are the first things potential customers and clients will focus on.

For black novices in the business world, that is probably doubly true.

There's an ugly little term used by some, both in and out of the black community, to describe how work is done. That term is "nigger rigged." It's the concept of something being shabbily slapped together to make it work. As a black business owner you constantly fight the bias that what you do is not going to be as professional as a white person doing the same thing.

And unfortunately, most black business owners will tell you that it is often blacks who will come to that conclusion quicker than whites will. Additionally, many black entrepreneurs will tell you that you don't have as long a learning curve in developing a solid reputation—one strike can take you out.

Regardless of the color of who you need to impress, you need to calculate the impact of the impression you make on others.

"I believe that being black is still more of a negative during initial encounters with some clients," Johnson says. "I feel that in most situations I can minimize the negative effects, however, I have to exert more time and energy to do so, whereas a white company or person can devote more of their energy towards the task. If you compare the two over time, I have to work harder. I accept that and prepare myself accordingly."

Which leads to the next quality to cultivate for blacks who want to make their way in the world following the path of the Emperor—the quality of integrity.

There are people out there who equate cashing in on the next get-rich-quick scheme with that of running your own business.

Following the path of the Emperor is about having the integrity to do it right—it's about putting the other qualities of leadership, organization and research ability into creating a new business.

A certain inherent commitment to integrity comes with the decision to leave Corporate America to start your own business. The mere pride of wanting to not embarrass yourself in front of your former co-workers and bosses can often keep you on track.

"The personality and character traits that served me well were: kindness, fairness and respect to all who came my way," says Johnson. "I consciously treated people differently, but strived to treat everyone fairly and equitably."

Being the Ultimate Boss Has Its Cost. But the Price Can Be Right

For all the ways we Americans can criticize working for "The Man" or working as a nameless cog, it does provide a certain framework for knowing the right way to operate in the business world when you're the person who owns the business. It's the workplace equivalent of "home training"—you can tell the adults whose families raised them to operate with good manners in public versus the people who act like they were raised by wolves.

Robert Williams Adams is an insurance and benefits advocate and special investigator. Adams is the Owner & Chief Advocate of Life Claim Solutions (LCS), an insurance and benefits consulting company in Philadelphia, PA.

Prior to starting his own business, Adam spent 13 years in Corporate America as an insurance and benefits Administrator and corporate troubleshooter for various areas of insurance.

"I had a plan to enter the corporate structure and learn and educate myself on all aspects of the insurance and benefits business," Adams said. "I targeted, studied and obtained relevant advanced designations (not degrees), that taught me the practical applications of how insurance and benefits worked for people at the time when they need the benefits the most."

For those who enter Corporate America and then decide to leave it, it can provide a good education. And combined with your own sense of integrity, that can be a useful combination.

Adams said that he has always had a strong sense of conviction to ethics and justice and has considered being an entrepreneur since he was a child.

"I have ... always been an avid reader, researcher and fact-finder," Adams said.

Adams says he views obstacles as "challenges to see what I am really made of on the inside."

"I always encounter obstacles in my business, but ultimately persistence, tenacity, intrepidness, and great research preparation are the keys to victory and success," Adams said.

Adams said that being black has required him to keep his awareness high pertaining to the struggles that blacks have traditionally faced and still face in the business world. He believes being black still plays a huge role in his career path.

Giving Back as an Expectation

One of the key considerations for blacks who decided to follow the path of the Emperor is that successful black leaders and entrepreneurs are expected to give back to the community. While there are obviously plenty of whites who do volunteer and charity work, for the most part, blacks who "make it" feel pressured to give back to the community.

For example, a 2004 study called "Pathways for Change: Philanthropy Among African-Americans, Latinos and Asian-Americans in the New York Metropolitan Region" showed that the median level of giving for blacks was $5,000 compared to the median level of $4,000 for all donors in the state of New York.

In particular, blacks who rely on the black community for their customer or client base are especially instilled on the moral responsibility to give back to the community. Even if you didn't grow up in the "hood," you're expected not just to succeed but to share the success with the black community—particularly the disenfranchised segment.

Adams gladly takes on that role.

"I have left white Corporate America completely in my mind, heart, and soul. I believe that our people should have clear-cut goals and objectives in our dealings with … Corporate America," Adams said. "Our top priority should be to obtain the education, training and experience from these corporations, and use the access …. to then turn our skills inward to our race and help our people as much as we possibly can."

Adams believes that black entrepreneurs should use their skills and talents to implement positive change and socio-economic development in our communities.

Both Johnson and Adams, while finding great meaning and service in the businesses they've created, are travelers who probably would have eventually built an idea from scratch and turned it into a business.

Guided By the Sheer Love of the Task

However, the other kind of black traveler who takes the path of the Emperor is the person who has a specific calling that can best be carried out as the owner of his or her own business.

One of the most famous black travelers to follow the path of the Emperor is Madame C. J. Walker. Walker liked experimenting with potions to figure out how to best have her hair turn out right. All the experimenting turned into a whole line of hair care products which made her a millionaire long before the days of Oprah counting zeros in her net worth. When Walker died at the age of 52 in 1919, her life accomplishments remained as an inspiring testament to how a deep passion can turn into a profitable business.

If you know that you have a love of leadership and an underlying love of a hobby or past time then maybe you should explore how that might be a business.

For the woman who not only loves to cook but also enjoys making up recipes and creating an environment in which to enjoy her delicacies, opening her own restaurant may be the right thing for her.

One of my editors also suggests that other choices for someone who likes to cook might include having a mail order business, bake and design food gifts, open a bakery or kitchen or open a cooking school.

The point is not to give an exhaustive list, because if it's your passion that burns inside you then it's your individual responsibility to figure out exactly how to express it because the choice is what must move and sustain you.

Because while a brother or sister who likes to burn in the kitchen can find ways to do all these things in Corporate America, such as be a chef in someone else's restaurant or for a corporation's cafeteria, that may not be the best choice for the entrepreneurial spirit.

Dwight D. Eisenhower once said, "Pull the string and it will follow wherever you wish. Push it, and it will go nowhere at all."

Ultimately, finding yourself pulled by doing something you love may be the heart of why one pursues the path of the Emperor in the first place.

What Does It Look Like to Follow the Path of the Emperor?

Long and/or conventional hours. You may think you work long hours when you have a job in Corporate America, but when you own a business then the long hours, the unconventional hours come whether the money is coming in or not.

Following the path of the Emperor also means that you sometimes have to be the jack-of-all trades to keep everything running. For example, on some days, you might be required to do the payroll, be the plumber and attempt human resources even when none of those roles has anything to do with the expertise your business is based on.

What resources do you need to consider before taking on the path of the Emperor?

The first resource you have to start with is yourself. Can you really rely on yourself to be your best, first, last and most reliable resource? Will you have the physical, emotional and spiritual energy, stamina and drive to take on starting your own business and sustaining your own business?

If you do, then you have to ask yourself if you have the emotional support from the people who matter. Has your spouse or significant other signed on to this or do they think you're crazy for leaving the so-called security of Corporate America? If you have children who depend on you for financial support and time, have you done the analysis of how this will affect them.

I think many people who contemplate starting their own business look to the concrete resources first—money, location, clients or customers.

The first place to start is with sitting still with yourself to see if you have the mentality to work for yourself and run a business.

If you do it the other way around, you take unnecessary risks.

I'm all about taking risks when it's a considered one based on strong internal principles. But leaping into starting a business when more than half of them fail within the first year is not something to take lightly, particularly if you don't have the resources to cushion you if you take a tumble.

Once you've decided that you have the mentality to take the path of the Emperor what do you do next?

Researching the Path of the Emperor

If you want to start a business doing something that someone else is doing, it would be a good idea to pick the brains of some of those people.

Some people might worry about exposing themselves to potential competitors, but so what? At the time you're gathering research you will rarely be true competition to anyone but yourself.

The important point, however, is to keep your questions focused on general information gathering since I do think people can get skittish when questioned too directly and personally about their livelihood. For example, I think asking, "How would you recommend going about finding financing from local sources?" is a safer bet to ask than, "So, which bank loaned you money and what did you use as collateral?"

Black business owners frequently find themselves in the situation of having other blacks presume that anything can be asked of a brother or sister. Well, it can't. You can't even if it's a relative or close friend unless they've given you the green light to ask whatever you want or need to.

Also, by collecting research you'll be doing one of the key components of having a successful business—networking.

Networking is nothing more than rubbing elbows and sharing information with those who can help propel a career or business forward. In the beginning, especially at the information gathering stage, you may feel you have nothing to share of value with others.

But I believe that just sharing your goodwill until you do have something more concrete and/or valuable to offer can be a significant step to take. It's a form of professional karma—we all like to be admired and supported in our endeavors. Just the very act of seeking someone's advice is something of value they will remember down the line because it shows that you find value in what they do.

Another good step is seeing if you can contact any and every organization that might be related to the business you plan to start. While black organizations, such as your local Black Chamber of Commerce, the local NAACP and Urban League chapters offer good places to start, also follow up with or start with the major organizations, particularly your local Chamber of Commerce.

The local Chamber of Commerce and the Better Business Bureau may have actual literature to send you for free or a small price to give you guidance on how to start a business.

As part of your researching, make sure you have obtained an email address if you don't already have one. Even if you don't own a computer, borrow a friend's or use one at the public library and obtain an address with Yahoo, MSN, Earthlink or some other free service. The importance of an email address cannot be underestimated in our modern times where it is expected for networking purposes.

Also, truly brainstorm. Think of each and every kind of group that might be remotely connected to the kind of business you want to start. If you have to, flip through the Yellow Pages, play on the Internet plugging in different searches to figure out who to contact for more information.

When you think about starting your own business most of the thinking and planning has to happen before you make the first dollar. That's why you have to think wide, not narrow.

Laws and Financing Issues to Consider

Another issue to consider when deciding to start your own business is the subject of local zoning laws, depending on what you want to do. You especially need to keep this in mind if you plan on running your business out of your home, especially if there will be any customer or client traffic. A call to your local zoning department and business license department of your city or municipality should clear up any confusion.

Going the route of calling the Chamber of Commerce should lead you to obtaining information on how to obtain a small business loan. Not every new business owner would necessarily qualify or want one if they do, but it's always better to know your options. Using them is another option.

Contacting the Small Business Administration is a great source to contact about loan programs and other information. Additionally, checking the weekly business section of your local newspaper will let you know of area seminars and workshops regarding starting a business.

It's important to remember that starting a business requires almost as much education as learning a skill as an artist or pursuing a professional degree. It's a path that is being taken by many others, so there is a wealth of expertise to uncover in your backyard once you start seeking it out.

- The traits of one following the path of the Emperor include wanting to lead, having a high degree of organizational ability, being a good researcher and cultivating an innate sense of integrity.

- Resources particularly important for one following the path of the Emperor include self, loved ones, researching the experiences of others who have taken the same or similar path and obtaining the right degree of financing.

- Challenges of following the path of the Emperor include learning to be a jack-of-all-trades, long and unconventional hours, stress from the high demands of clients, expectations of giving back to the community and financial challenges.

Chapter Four

Path of the Artisan

Happiness lies in the joy of achievement and the thrill of creative effort.
—Franklin Roosevelt

Signpost: This chapter is about pursing a livelihood based on the creation of and the making of money from art. Art is an expansive term and includes music, the visual arts, dance, acting and the kind of endeavors based on talent and skill.

Is Pursuing Art the Pursuit for You?

Next to avoiding or leaving Corporate America to start a new business, the other area of non-traditional income for black Americans has typically been that of entertainment.

The unfortunate legacy of our reality as black Americans is that even at the height of open bigotry and discrimination, white folks have always been willing to let blacks entertain them. So, for those blacks who had the talent and desire to express their art as performers, a few doors were opened to them. A few, not all.

Now, I think the path of the Artisan for today's black person encompasses far more than singing and dancing. For those travelers who choose to follow the path of the Artisan, true diversity of talent is represented—music, producing, writing, visual arts, performance arts. It includes any kind of art that someone produces from pure passion, desire and talent that can be transmuted into a cash stream.

One could argue that pursuing sports as a career path would fall under the path of the Artisan. Sports are about innate ability and for some athletes it's about actual passion for the sport. But in terms of making a livelihood, much of obtaining success in the professional sports arena comes from recruitment by teams at an early age. Therefore, it doesn't quite fit into the same category since most professional athletes have not stepped away from Corporate America or have seriously considered entering it.

I also admit that I hold the bias that professional athletes have only so long to enjoy and profit from the bloom on the rose. They've got to get while the getting is good in terms of making money from their sport while they are at their physical peak. In basketball, for example, the age of 39 is ancient for a professional in the NBA. But a writer, a painter, a composer, an actor, can create a livelihood for themselves in to their 80s if God's willing and the creek don't rise.

According to the Department of Labor, more than half of all artists and related workers (which mainly included visual artists) were self-employed, which is eight times the proportion for all professional and related occupations. Therefore, in part, the path of the Artisan is similar to the path of the Emperor in that you are your own boss and similar to the path of the Hermit (explored in the next chapter) in that your livelihood is a solo enterprise.

One thing that is important to note about the path of the Artisan, as the above statistic illustrates, is that there are ways to pursue art within Corporate America. For example, graphic artists who work for a design company or copywriters who work for an advertising executive.

The focus of this chapter is on those black travelers who pursue art as a vocation outside of Corporate America.

Earlier, I talked about the difference between opting out and copping out. Unfortunately for those who follow the path of the Artisan, in the black community, almost everyone else will think you are copping out if they don't see an instant flow of income attached to your art.

Unless there is a huge and immediate influx of cash, it's hard for the people in your life who love you to take seriously the idea of you making a "real" living from art.

It's understandable when you view it in the context of fairly recent history. The Civil Rights movement was fought on the basis of making concrete gains of equality in our society and oftentimes equality and power are associated with how much money one makes.

For relatives who can remember the existence of Jim Crow laws— state-sanctioned discrimination—or who remember how difficult it was for a black to get the most entry level job in major corporations, the speculative nature of art can seem frivolous at best.

In all fairness to those who care about you, it can be difficult to make a living following the path of the Artisan. However, difficult is not even close to impossible.

How do you decide if following the path of the Artisan is for you? It's true that a passion for art may just be a hobby or it could be that your passion could be your life's work.

Later in the book I have a chapter on being a part-time traveler while still having one foot in Corporate America. The Artisan is best served by wading into their passion part-time, especially if you're already gainfully employed in Corporate America.

It may sound like I'm advocating playing it safe and timid. No, it's just that art as a way of making money is something that requires others to find it of value.

Therefore, the very fact that you may love creating art doesn't necessarily mean that you are good at it. Harsh but true. Actually, the more accurate thing to say is that whether you think you're good at it or not is irrelevant, it's whether the marketplace is willing to pay you for it.

Art truly is a situation where beauty rests in the eye of the beholder. When one follows the path of the Emperor—starts their own business—he or she usually peddles a product or a service for which a market demand exists or for which a demand can be artificially created with clever marketing. In general, however, the trick for those on the path of the Emperor is convincing a large enough base of people to pick your business over all the other businesses offering the same thing.

For example, if you start a business as an air conditioning repair person, you've picked a service where there is an objective demand. People all over the country have air conditioners and those units—window and central—and they break down. To build a business however, you have to compete with all the other people who also fix air conditioners. But with enough time and money put into advertising, marketing and word-of-mouth by satisfied customers, you can get your share of the market. It might be one percent, it might be 70 percent but a share is yours to grab.

But for someone who decides to make modern art from the broken parts of air conditioners, it becomes significantly more dicey that someone will decide that the art is good enough to merit a price tag.

Art is different. People don't need art. At least not in the same way that they need products and services. There are people who may get no greater pleasure than that derived from reading a great book, gazing at an exquisite watercolor, viewing a moving film. But those people seek to have their hearts and souls fed by the spiritual.

Unfortunately, for those of us who are artists, what we produce may not necessarily be touching anyone's spiritual center.

Answering the Call of the Muse

Ed Hamilton is an amazing sculptor who lives in Louisville, Kentucky. His work has included the African American Civil War Memorial in Washington, D.C., the Amistad Memorial in New Haven, Connecticut, a statue of Booker T. Washington for Hampton University and a statue of heavy weight champion Joe Louis for the City of Detroit.

Hamilton, of Ed Hamilton Studios, Inc., avoided traditional Corporate America and worked for years as a teacher on the high school level, including creating a sculpture program for Kentucky Community College. He said he worked many other jobs to make ends meet.

"My path started with two very strong willed art teachers who saw talent and helped to hone it. Four years of art school, teaching and then the meeting of a sculptor that would change my life forever," Hamilton says. "Working along side a full time sculptor for six years allowed me to learn the business of sculpting and meet those persons of influence that would help me later."

"Corporate America was never on my radar as a way of making my living. But in a small way I am connected with Corporate America just by virtue of my incorporated status and being in business."

Pursuing the path of the Artisan requires similar qualities to those who follow the path of the Emperor. In part, it requires that same gut-level desire to be in charge of your path.

There's a saying in the younger black community, "Don't hate the player, hate the game." Black travelers—regardless of which path they choose—are those who attempt to create their own game.

Sometimes that calling, that desire, comes from something innate. And at times, it's fed by being raised with the mentality that one should sculpt their own future. Hamilton quickly attributes his parents for helping to nurture his inner artistic spirit.

"Surely the paths that my mother and father were on helped to seal my fate as to being in business for myself. They were self-employed, owned their own business and went to work everyday. I saw this and realized how important it is to be dedicated to your dream of controlling your own destiny," said Hamilton.

In terms of how his race has played a role in pursuing the path of the Artisan, Hamilton sees how that has shaped his unique experience as a full-time, professional artist.

"[Being black] was not a hindrance; actually in some cases it has been helpful. When the major commissions began, they were African-Americans and it just felt right that I, an African-American, would be the one to bring to life their stories that have been left out of the history books, for we did not write those books. So all of this could not have happened at a better time," Hamilton said.

Hamilton touches on one aspect of taking the path of the Artisan and finding success, which is always nurturing your skill to be prepared for good timing when it comes along.

The Importance of Nurturing Your Talent

So, how does a black traveler decide whether their art will put money in their pockets to go with the inner glow that comes from creating?

One of the first ways to decide that may be to formally or semi-formally study your craft. Taking classes or joining artist groups can put you in touch with people who can give you feedback. As Hamilton learned, having a positive, trustworthy mentor or set of mentors can be a huge advantage.

However, the emphasis has to be on studying the craft and not merely obtaining validation. Fellow artists and wannabe artists can be notoriously adept at undermining the confidence of someone with talent who may be a bit insecure about that talent.

One of the best ways to use the feedback from people you study your craft with is to pay more attention to the specific craft related suggestions rather than the general subjective comments on whether something is "good" or "bad".

For example, when Pete (real name not used) joined a writing group that met once a week to critique the novels in progress of each of the members of the writing group, Pete received excellent advice and input on how to properly write point-of-view to tell the story. He received invaluable feedback regarding how to handle first person versus third person and how to be conscious of what details are pertinent depending on which viewpoint is used in a story. However, when Pete began getting positive feedback from publishing houses regarding his submitted work, his critique group got cattier and the comments focused more on value judgments of whether his work was good and less on the concrete suggestions he had initially received.

Julia Cameron, author of one of my favorite books called "The Artist's Way", talks about people in the life of an artist called "crazymakers" who unknowingly (and sometimes knowingly) sabotage the work or confidence of an artist because it is a threat to the fact that the crazymaker fails to address their own artistic urges and resents that you pursue yours.

For a black traveler on the path of the Artisan, being on the lookout for crazymakers can be even more necessary because our well of role models may be shallow or seemingly non-existent. Therefore, the lack of positive feedback or reinforcement may not be loud enough to drown out the chorus of crazymakers.

Crazymakers will say things like: "Baby, that picture is pretty but when you gonna get a real job?" or "Honey, writing is a nice hobby but you need to stop playing and apply for that job I circled for you in the classifieds. That would make me feel so much better."

The unsettling thing is that our crazymakers sometimes don't have anything different to say beyond what our genuinely supportive loved ones with no underlying negative motivations are also saying to us. For example, a well meaning parent may question whether you can truly make a living from making jewelry because they genuinely have never met anyone who has done that and thus are worried about you being able to pay your mortgage. A crazymaker, on the otherhand, may ask for no other reason than to rattle you, keep you tied to a life that best benefits them and just generally be indifferent and callous about the fact that they may be undermining you.

Learning the distinction between well placed concern and unfounded crazymaking is a life long lesson in developing good instincts and creating solid emotional boundaries.

Singer Anita Baker was told at least once early in her career that she couldn't sing. Thankfully, she didn't listen to those crazymakers and kept right on singing.

While following the path of the Artisan is a seed planted by the inherent creativity of a particular traveler, the true creativity comes from melding the desire to create with the need to have a roof over your head. It ties back to what I wrote in the introduction about Maslow's hierarchy of needs—it's hard to think about those higher needs of self-actualization and creativity when you can't put enough cash together for the rent due next week.

Staying in Corporate America Can Help Pay for the Path

Therefore, as a matter of both actual and artistic survival, some black travelers who follow the path of the Artisan realize they can not afford to be narrow-minded in how they approach their art.

For example, a black traveler who loves to paint beautiful, heart thumping oil landscapes might want nothing more than to paint all day, have people pay him thousands of dollars per painting and live happily ever after as a world renowned artist.

While that could very well be a viable goal for the people who have the divine combination of talent, luck and opportunity, intermediate steps may be necessary.

There are some people who can work in a corporate environment that has nothing to do with their art until their art for pay takes off.

Monica Jackson, a Topeka, Kansas based writer of black romances and literature, has had several novels published by one of the largest publishers of black romance novels. However, it was only until she reached near double digits of published novels that she can actually write full time for a living. Until that point, she was working hard as a nurse. Jackson says that not many multi-published black writers who she knows are able to devote themselves exclusively to their art. One of the most popular writers in the genre still works full-time in the health care industry.

Some artists, however, are only going to be happy if they can exhibit some version of their art in the workplace.

A writer, for example, who craves writing spy novels for a living might need to work for the communication department of a major corporation writing business plans. A sketch artist who dreams of an art show in SoHo in New York City may need to settle for drawing advertising copy in Dallas, Texas. An actor who aims to win an

Oscar and a Tony in one lifetime might find herself having to nurture her acting chops while teaching high school drama class or working in one of those restaurants where they practically sing your food to your table.

M. LaVora Perry is the author of children's books as well as an editor and web designer. Prior to working as a writer, Perry was the first black greeting card writer for American Greetings, the world's largest publicly owned greeting card company.

"In time, in addition to writing cards [for American Greetings], I began to edit them," Perry said, who was the lead concept person for the In Rhythm African-American card line, innovative for its time.

"When I was first hired by [American Greeting] I was pregnant, so I came on as a part-timer, working three days a week," Perry said, saying that she stayed for seven years in part-time status, part of it at home, but often working the equivalent of a full-time job. Perry said she didn't mind putting in the extra hours in Corporate America while also raising her three children. "I really enjoyed doing my best. I felt I owed it to the company because they started me on my professional writing career."

While working in Corporate America, Perry realized she helped serve as an agent for change in allowing the company to see a working mother efficiently handle a "flex" schedule while doing award-winning work.

Perry realizes that not every black person who works wants to work for themselves or in an unconventional way. So, in paving a new path for herself she helped to pave a path for the blacks who do want to work in Corporate America.

"[My former company] hired three additional African-Americans into [my department] since I first came aboard," Perry said. "Knowing that I would not remain a company employee for life, one of my goals had always been to replace myself with two other people of color in my department whenever I finally left. I'd like to think I contributed to bringing about some of the changes that have occurred in the company."

Perry believes Corporate America is something that requires a particular kind of fit for anyone, particularly a black employee.

"The rules often did not make sense to me and I stepped beyond them without even realizing I was doing it sometimes—I was just being myself," Perry said.

"By 2002 the desire that I'd long held to publish a children's story I'd originally written in 1998 grew very strong. I was determined to have my book, 'Taneesha's Treasures of the Heart,' published by the end of that year no matter what. When it was turned down by publishers several times, I decided to publish it myself. With three young children and the job of preparing a manuscript for publication, I felt I did not have the time to also work at [my job in Corporate America]. As it was, when I had big projects, I already frequently pulled all-nighters."

When she decided to resign to write her book, Perry relied on the support of her husband, her parents and her retirement fund.

"I took the leap," Perry summarizes.

Along with people, Perry said one of her support systems in deciding to pursue her path as a writer, was her faith. Perry attributes being a practicing Buddhist to helping her develop the confidence to set out on the path she's on. Other qualities have also helped.

"I really believe I can do whatever I set my mind to, and I can be focused. This can be an attribute or a hindrance. Sometimes I am so focused on what I want that I don't see the ramifications of my actions on other people—or even myself," Perry said. "However, the up side of my single-mindedness is that once I set my sights on a goal and burn its outcome into my psyche, I can march toward its completion indefinitely—I just don't quit until I get to the finish line."

Perry acknowledges that race is an issue in pushing toward her path but she doesn't let it define her approach.

"I know first hand that racism is a very real entity. But I don't allow that fact, or the racism that I feel I have personally encountered, to prevent me from doing what I need to do," said Perry. Perry said she lives by the credo she once heard from Oprah Winfrey, "The best defense is success."

Putting All the Pieces in Place to Succeed as an Artist

Artistic expression can be as individual as the individual seeking it out. And when that is combined with trying to make a living out of it, it can get complicated.

One question to ask yourself regarding your ability to take the path of the Artisan is, does the location of where you live lend itself to authentically supporting your art?

For example, if acting is your art, does the venue of your art really match the venue located on your driver's license? If you long for film work, are you willing to make the move to Hollywood? Or if your heart's desire is Broadway, are you willing to relocate to New York City if you don't already live there?

If your art can be done on a less ambitious scale then don't think that's easier because your area is smaller. Local theatre requires talent and tenacity to break into also. Getting your art in shows can be no less difficult in Manhattan, Kansas than in Manhattan, New York.

Cecilia Aderonke, an actress from Kansas City, Missouri, mentioned earlier who now lives in New York City, had to ask herself those hard questions. While she was getting acting parts and singing gigs in Kansas City, including playing the role of Billie Holliday, she knew she was going to best carry out her path by taking a permanent bite out of the Big Apple.

"Your biggest support system is yourself," Aderonke said. "When you move in the realm of genius, it really is about your self and your spirit."

Although Aderonke has two degrees and comes from a strong, middle-class family, she was willing to work herself to the bone at jobs ranging from housecleaning to waiting tables to save the money she needed for her New York move.

Her focus now, as she settles into her beautiful Harlem studio apartment, is on making the right contacts, sending out headshots and her acting resume, polishing up her demos and basically enjoying the life she creates for herself as a New York City actress and singer.

The point is that you must be willing while following the path of the Artisan to have your circumstances support your art or be willing to change your circumstances.

Besides determining talent and dealing with the possible limitations of location, the other big area to consider for a traveler pursuing the path of the Artisan is assembling your support system.

Earlier, I visited the subject of seeking feedback to determine if your art is good and has independent market value. However, if you decide to take it to the next level to actually use your art to make a livelihood then you need other kinds of support.

Later I will discuss family support for those who avoid or leave Corporate America. But for those who follow the path of the Artisan, the personal support can be particularly dicey.

For one, most art takes time. To create something– to write, to paint, to sculpt, to rehearse, to film, to design, to plan—takes time away from friends and family. At least in their minds it does.

Perry, the writer of children's books, realized that the key to the life she has embarked on is one of balance. Perry said she has had to learn how to let things slide, for example, some business matters, so that her family can get the nurturing and time they need.

"The biggest obstacle is money. I am not independently wealthy, yet I have embarked on a project—publishing and promoting books—that is costly. The second biggest obstacle is time—I've got little ones at home that need all of me, a lot of the time."

The Internal and External Benefits of Pursuing the Path of the Artisan

Art can be a lot like exercise—people usually cite time constraints as the main reason they don't do it without realizing that it creates time, more energy and better health to be spent on all those other priorities in life that require your presence.

Like exercise, the benefits from pursuing your art as an artist are internal first and it takes a while for the rest of the world to see the external benefits.

Often times, unless loved ones see some immediate payoff, they will view your art as a hobby and not take it very seriously. Even if they see you making money from it, they will still expect you to find a "real" job.

And truth is that's not a completely negative reaction since it does take money to support your art, pay for your art and give you the peace of mind to pursue your art.

Hamilton, the sculptor, says, "I think the main obstacle that I have had to overcome and in some cases even today, is earning power.

Art is a business but it also is something that I would do even if I had not pursued it as my vocation. One has to be on top of things and as a small corporation I am well aware of the pitfalls and hoops we have to go through to make all of our financial ends work for us. So for me it had to be the money!"

In the end, if you can successfully gather the resources together to take the path of the Artisan, it's a rewarding road to travel. For those who truly find joy from what they do, there's no other path in the mind and heart to follow. It's indeed the Yellow Brick Road.

Art Is A Business and You As the Artist Are the Product

In some ways, as stated before, pursuing the path of the Artisan is very similar to pursuing the path of the Emperor, a black traveler who starts their own business.

If you're talking about making a living as an artist, then you're art—as well as yourself through your artistic talent—is the product. And like any product you sell you have to become a jack-of-all-trades who can ensure your resources are managed properly, your support system is in place and the challenges of producing your art balance out the business end of making sure it sells.

The main challenge in pursuing the path of the Artisan is having to worry about the business end of producing your art—marketing, showcasing, managing, scheduling, taxes, space and equipment; not to mention money and other related issues.

Part of the challenge may be in having to juggle your art with some job unrelated to or only marginally related to your art.

Being an artist—similar to being a business owner—is about pacing. It's about juggling long, erratic hours and constant internal motivation to succeed in a way that doesn't unduly compromise your art or burn you out.

- Pursuing the path of the Artisan is about aligning your creative spirit with the part of you that can be focused, and build a career.

- The benefits of the path of the Artisan include taking your talents and creative passions and creating a career.

- The challenges of pursuing the path of the Artisan are making money from your art, building sufficient family support during the sparse periods and balancing the time and energy needed to create or cultivate your art with the time and energy necessary to make sure it generates an income.

Chapter Five

The Path of the Hermit

So vain is the belief that the sequestered path has fewest flowers.
—Thomas Doubleday

Signpost: The path of the Hermit is for the black employee in Corporate America who likes or doesn't mind the work but doesn't like the structure of working in a conventional environment. The person following the path of the Hermit is an independent contractor who does not limit him or herself to one employer, but rather does contract work for multiple companies.

Contrasting Life of an Employee to the Life of the Independent Contractor

The path of the Hermit is for the black traveler who wants to work more of the solo life. The most frequently used terms to describe the person who takes the path of the Hermit include freelancer, contract employee or temp employee.

Approximately seven percent of the labor force is independent contractors with that number expecting to rise as high as 10 percent in the future.

What exactly is an independent contractor, which is the general term I will be using to describe the path of the Hermit?

Let's start by talking about the job of the typical employee in Corporate America because that provides the best contrast to describing how the position of independent contractor works.

An employee has one employer. The independent contractor is their own employer. An employee basically is hired for an indefinite period of time. An independent contractor usually works for a discrete, specific period of time. An employer determines the duties and method of performance for an employee. An independent contractor agrees to a specific duty or set of duties and determines the method of performance.

The negatives about taking the path of the Hermit can be the following: you have to arrange for your own benefits, you might miss the camaraderie of having co-workers, you may have irregular work schedules and workplaces and you lack the concrete Corporate America identity that most people are encouraged to pursue.

That last issue is not one to take lightly. Many of us black folks get a lot of our identity from saying we've worked at the plant for 22 years or have a position with Corporation XYZ or that we have an interview next week with Big Company.

It's somewhat understandable. Blacks are still a race of people who have a significant population that can remember Jim Crow and other organized forms of bigotry. We can remember when all doors were slammed to us except for the most menial of positions. Regardless of what age we are, there is not one black person in the country who doesn't have some older relative who has painful stories of what opportunities and positions where blatantly denied them. Therefore, the security of finding a good job in a respectable place was not an insignificant accomplishment.

The reality however for all Americans, not just black Americans, is that there is no such thing anymore as corporate job security. Between downsizing and laws that don't ensure job security and outsourcing, very few of us can count on receiving a gold watch when we retire. In fact, very few of us actually retire in the old-fashioned sense of the word—many of us just keep on working until the heart stops working and we have the ultimate retirement in a burial plot.

Those who choose to live the life of the independent contractor must accept the realities of an unsure work relationship.

Doing the Work But Deciding How You Do It

For many who follow the path of the Hermit, it's worth it to design their own workday on their own terms. One of the beauties of this approach, for example, is that to the extent you don't like a certain employer or supervisor it ends up being only a temporary situation.

Variety is a quality you must particularly appreciate to follow the path of the Hermit as a black traveler. If you like interacting with varied types of people whose roster of names is always changing, you'll like being an independent contractor. If you don't mind operating in a variety of environments and mixing up the quality and quantity of stresses you deal with, you will appreciate well this life.

The path of the Hermit is similar to the path of the Emperor in that you are most likely focusing on an expertise that tends to have a certain value attached to it in the marketplace. The life of an independent contractor, however, usually involves slicing a segment of the work done in Corporate America and doing it for pay.

For example, a black traveler who decides to quit her job and open up her own clothing store is following the path of the Emperor. The business may be selling clothes but all the factors of the business, whether related to clothes or not, are equally important to the actual selling of the clothes. You have to be concerned about the facilities, the licensing, the employees, taxes and marketing, just like other retail clothing businesses.

If you're the independent contractor whose only job is to make a certain amount of dresses in a limited amount of time, it's not your job to worry about any of the other aspects of the business. In fact, as soon as you are done making your order of dresses as an independent contractor for Company A you may turn around and make another batch of dresses for Company B.

That's one of the best aspects of being an independent contractor. As long as you're not violating any contract provisions, you don't have to worry about exhibiting company loyalty.

Another aspect of taking the path of the Hermit is the need for variety—they just like doing temporary work and don't have any particular expertise that moves them. There are several national companies who have a whole roster of temp employees who wait for a telephone call that tells them when and where to show up.

With these temp agencies people are free to accept or turn down assignments at their leisure without the problems that come with traditional employment.

Hermits are Internally Motivated

In addition to the love of variety, another quality that someone has to have in order to follow the path of the Hermit is the ability to be internally motivated.

When one works for Corporate America much of the motivation is external and spelled out for you by virtue of the fact that you got hired and you're expected to go to work every day.

Day in, day out, except when you're on vacation or out sick, the expectation from your boss is that you show up every day until you quit or get fired. In addition to regular paychecks, life in Corporate America is littered with carrots that your boss dangles in front of you to keep you interested in full-time employment. Those perks include end-of-year bonuses, annual raises, promise of promotion and other perks crafted by Corporate America.

Temp employees or independent contractors, on the other hand, decide when they are going to work to a certain extent, so they have to be motivated to seek out the next job. Granted, wanting to keep yourself in electricity, water and gas is motivation enough. But it still requires a certain internal discipline to line up the next job or project while working on the one you're finishing up.

Rebecca J. Shepherd is a small business consultant who does freelance writing, particularly for grants and technical work. Prior to doing this work, Shepherd worked in Corporate America for eight years in the public relations and advertising field and as a childcare specialist for 16 years. At one point she followed the path of the Emperor by owning a daycare center for five years.

Being injured in a catastrophic car wreck which left her disabled changed things for Shepherd dramatically. She decided to create a work situation for herself that was more conducive to her physical adjustments.

"I have a very outgoing and intuitive personality, a very strong and dynamic presence combined with an ability to communicate very well with others," Shepherd said, seeing those as among the many traits that have helped her to succeed.

In terms of family support, like many black families, Shepherd said she was steered toward the "safe" profession of teaching. She said that once she struck out on her own to create a new path for herself, her family began to support her as they saw her make a go of it. Primarily she sees the bulk of her obstacles as being health-related, and she believes she can persevere over those also.

Whether working directly in Corporate America or as someone who does independent contract work, Shepherd knows that race can be an issue.

"In some ways [race] has worked to my advantage, particularly in the RFP (Request for Proposals) and RFB (Request for Bids) areas. These areas are highly competitive and don't have a lot of black female entrepreneurs, so when the opportunity arises, most times I am received favorably, because they need the minority contractor," Shepherd said. "In other ways it makes me have to work harder, sometimes 16 hours a day. More often than not, because I am a black and female entrepreneur, they question my skills and credibility."

"I am definitely a Corporate America drop out. When I worked in Advertising, I was on the fast track, quickly moving from entry level to Executive Management, but the politics and I didn't mix!," Shepherd said. "I was considered a rebel from day one because of my strong ties to rank and file. I was not willing to compromise my values to make that big salary."

Shepherd said that for her, the life she has chosen for herself works more so than twisting herself into the pretzel that traditional Corporate America required.

"I have flexible hours, I can work from home," Shepherd said. "It allows me to take only the clients I feel I have a viable service or product to benefit the community. So I can work from a position of being community motivated as opposed to being profit motivated."

Shepherd said her life as an independent contractor both feeds her spirit and allows her to take into account her physical limitations.

"And with my disability, I don't lose money when I am sick, I work around it. And since I am my own boss and support staff, it allows me a lot of versatility in my tasks on a daily basis," Shepherd said. "I enjoy the work more because each project and client is different, as I work primarily with non-profits. And my freelance job of writing allows me the creative experience that is more fulfilling than any upper management position might afford."

Shepherd said she is the first to admit that the life she has created for herself on the path of the Hermit is not an easy one or for anyone attached to the conventional way of doing things. But she does believe that life as an independent contractor is in reach for all of us since this country was founded on the free enterprise system.

"Though it is not an easy task in the beginning, you will find in time that it is definitely worth the risk and the time to stay within the margins of your capabilities," Shepherd said. "Surround yourself with people smarter than yourself as you will need much counsel during this experience, especially other small business owners and entrepreneurs."

The Practical Aspects to Doing It On Your Own

One following the path of the Hermit also has to give thought to the practical aspects of working as a lone wolf.

The first issue is health insurance. If you work for yourself that means you do not have an employer who provides group health insurance. The burden is on you to seek out quotes and insurance from carriers who will provide it to you. Some who follow the path of the Hermit, especially the younger people, might be tempted to forgo health insurance to save money. But as anyone who has been afflicted with even the most minor health problem knows, that can be more costly in the end.

If you're leaving Corporate America to follow the path of the Hermit, a temporary measure to consider is COBRA (Consolidated Omnibus Budget Reconciliation Act of 1986). COBRA is a law that, among other things, requires employers to provide the temporary continuation of health insurance coverage at group rates. This can still be more expensive for you as a former employee than as a current employee since you are no longer having part of it paid for you. But it can be cheaper than obtaining individual coverage. Life insurance, however, is not covered under COBRA; and COBRA coverage is not indefinite.

Another thing to consider regarding benefits, however, is that in some cases after a temporary employee has worked for one employer for one year, an employer is required to offer the employee the same benefits offered to regular employees. Also, some temp agencies are large enough to offer group health insurance to individuals.

Going It Alone Can Still Be Done With Company

The ever changing structure of the workforce can be a good thing for those who want to follow the path of the Hermit but who truly don't want to go it alone. Several large, medium and small agencies exist that cater to people who want to be temporary, contract or independent contractors. Let me be more accurate—these agencies cater to the companies willing to pay the money to have an agency do all the work of providing them with temporary employees.

Many of these agencies specialize in certain things. For example, agencies that hire medical personnel, legal personnel or clerical workers. A look in your local Yellow Pages under employment agencies will point you in the right direction.

One benefit of those black travelers who decide to follow the path of the Hermit is that there exists a great market for those who don't want to do traditional employment. Many employers are increasingly relying on temporary employees because they are growing weary of how unreliable the workforce can be from their perspective.

While apartment hunting earlier this year, I met a white owner of a small business who said he doesn't even have employees anymore, he just uses people hired from a temporary service. In fact, he said that his highest paid executive, making more than $60,000 a year, was an employee through a temp agency.

Even though I had met many employers as employment defense attorney, this position from a business owner seemed kind of extreme.

"What about the loyalty and consistency that a regular workforce provides? What about people willing to bust their butts to get raises and promotions?

This business owner said he didn't have a problem with not having loyalty and consistency, that the turnover of the temp employees was no greater than when he had his own employees. Plus, he had the added advantage of not having to pay benefits and that replacing people he no longer liked was a lot less sticky.

This owner's position seemed awfully cold to me, even devoid of a little humanity. My viewpoint was further enhanced by his telling me the impetus that made him go from having a permanent workforce to a temporary workforce—he got sued for discrimination based on religion.

Even though there may have been nothing wrong with what this small business owner was doing (although without looking it up, my gut reaction was there were some holes in his analysis that might still open him up to liability), it just seemed sad for a whole lot of reasons. I am usually not one of those people who believe that a corporation should have some benign paternalistic influence over the lives of their employees. But it is unnerving that some employers could ease their burdens by just deciding that employees can be eliminated altogether.

That's one of the reasons why I do think that black travelers have to seriously contemplate the advantages of pursuing the path of the Hermit. These days, with a few exceptions, there isn't much long-term corporate loyalty on either side of the employer-employee line. However, it is still difficult for an individual to find him or her self taking that path.

As with all the other non-traditional paths to creating a livelihood, those who follow the paths of the Hermit may find the support from loved ones paper thin.

Because many of them will still be plowing single-mindedly through Corporate America, most of those loved ones will have a very difficult time understanding why you don't just seek a permanent job at one place. While even unsupportive loved ones can work up to understanding the allure of owning your own business (path of the Emperor) or the excitement of following your muse to have an artistic career (path of the Artisan), you will have an even more difficult time explaining that you just want a more independent existence.

Temp Work or Contract Work Is Done By Many

If people would see contract or temporary work as a viable option that does provide a little security of its own nature, there might be fewer unhappy people bouncing from one "permanent" job to another for short periods of time.

Bureau of Labor Statistics (BLS) data from 1999 indicated that employment in temporary help is now one fifth of employment in manufacturing. Another reason is the growth of the temporary help services industry. Employment in the temporary help services industry grew five times as fast as overall non-farm employment between 1972 and 1997—an average annual growth rate of 11% with this sector accounting for 20% of all employment growth by the 1990s. [From "The Effect of Work in the Temporary Help Industry" published by Urban Institute in October 2001].

The American Staffing Association says that there are more than 7,000 staffing (temp) agencies across the country that have been in existence more than one year.

According to the Bureau of Labor Statistics, in 2001, 8.6 million people defined themselves as independent contractors, 633,000 were contract company workers and 1.2 million were temp-agency workers.

To Work Alone, Reliability is More Important Not Less

One aspect or characteristic you must consider to decide whether to take the path of the Hermit is to decide whether you are reliable. Just because you don't have a full-time gig with one employer does not mean you have free rein to come and go as you please.

Having the option to work short-term or project oriented jobs does not mean that you can simply fail to show up when you want or behave any way you want in the workplace.

I know of a young black woman who worked for an employment agency that specialized in outsourcing medical assistants. One night she and another medical assistant got sassy with a supervisor. The other assistant was a full-time assistant at the facility. One of the young women got terminated that night for unprofessional behavior. Was it the full-time employee? No, it was the woman who worked for the agency. The agency no longer felt comfortable sending her out to other jobs so she was axed from the agency.

The sassy sistah with the temp agency got worse punishment than the employer's permanent employee because she had more independent responsibility and blew it. The permanent assistant was disciplined for her behavior but didn't lose her job because she had the long term history with her employer for this to be considered an incident that warranted another chance.

That's an example of why someone who pursues the path of the Hermit has to be hyper vigilant about their reliability. That's because it is far easier to get rid of someone who doesn't really work for you in the first place than a long-term employee.

Katie M. Wilkerson has recently moved from a lengthy career as a legal secretary to becoming a freelance sign language interpreter.

She started on the path by going back to school in her mid-30s to obtain a degree in Sign Language Interpreting. Wilkerson found that her path is based on what motivates her internally.

"I have always been interested in words and language. As a child, I read ferociously and still do to this day," Wilkerson said, who earlier this year left the legal secretary field to pursue her freelance status fulltime. "I have the kind of personality that lends to always wanting to help someone who may be less fortunate than I."

Wilkerson said that based on her family's background in education and ministry, she became fascinated with wanting to aid in the communication between the world of the deaf and the world of the hearing.

Additionally, she sees that the subculture of people who are both black and deaf are doubly in need of people like her.

"The black deaf community is screaming out for interpreters of color who understand their culture. There is a distinct 'deaf culture' but an even more distinct black deaf culture," Wilkerson said, passionate about the path she has chosen for her self. "Using white interpreters for functions that may be of a black cultural type such as a white interpreter at a NAACP meeting just does not feel right to them. Many black Deaf people would love to attend functions that are clearly of a black cultural type but do not feel comfortable with white interpreters."

One of the reasons she has gradually left Corporate America is that she has chosen a path that is both hard to break into and is not high-paying once you do.

"I actually have been blessed with mentors," Wilkerson said of the wealth of resources she has encountered in the sign language interpretation field. "But as to financial, well the sign language interpreting field is not one that pays a lot. Most interpreters starting out do not come out of school with a high enough certification level to go to work full-time. In order to get to that level of certification you must be able to hone your skills and the only way to do that is through on-the-job training and a whole lot of practice and study."

Wilkerson felt that she was lucky in her ability to pay for her dream. "I was one of the lucky people. At the time I went to school my [older] daughter also started college. I was able to receive grants to pay for most of my tuition; books and expenses were taken from my regular paycheck. We did a lot of the 'fun' things but we made it without too many financial setbacks."

The cost for her in pursuing this vocation are doubly high as a single parent who finds that a lot of her experience can be gained during daytime hours while she works her legal secretary job.

One of the attractions the field of sign language interpreter has for her is the extra flexibility of being a freelance interpreter instead of a fulltime employee.

"As a freelance interpreter I will be able to set my own hours," said Wilkerson. "I will be available to my youngest child when she needs me there to go to school activities, to attend tutoring sessions, etc."

Wilkerson, as many others have, notes that treatment, understanding and management of black folks in the workplace can be starkly different from that of her white, married counterparts, another reason why she seeks out the freelance life.

In the beginning of this book, I talked about how the whole idea of leaving or avoiding Corporate America, for some people, is about finding their passion. It's about finding personal meaning in what they do when they earn a living and not just holding down a job to exist.

That's why the example of Wilkerson is particularly instructive, because in addition to creating a new life for herself, she has become heavily involved in Deaf Advocacy, particularly for those who are both black and deaf.

"Sometimes, it is no more than writing a letter or finding information for deaf people. But most of the people I do this type of work for are black deaf people," Wilkerson said. "Many have no idea they cannot be fired just because they are deaf and many black deaf people are even more discriminated against than hearing black people. As you can see, this is an area that stands very close to my heart."

For those who choose a path, rather than fall into the Corporate way of life, it often times does end up being about something larger than just finding an alternate way of making a living.

One Can Be the Loneliest Number

Although following the path of the Hermit has many benefits, among the pitfalls are that people are used to folks having a traditional employer when it comes to matters like credit and proving your income.

Similar to the issues of those following the paths of the Emperor (entrepreneurship) or the Artisan (pursuing an artistic career) a person following the path of the Hermit needs to be particularly diligent about keeping financial records in order and possibly seeking the advice of a good accountant to make sure tax issues are properly handled.

Another challenge for one following the path of the Hermit is making sure that financial droughts are anticipated for times when project work does not come through or payment for work performed is extremely slow. One tip I've found that can be helpful is paying as many bills in advance as possible, for example paying rent or mortgage in advance if a significant sized check comes in or paying more than what is due on utility bills when possible.

As with all these paths out of Corporate America, the adjustments can be unique to individual situations and thus, the solutions will be too.

- To follow the path of the Hermit, you have to be the kind of black employee who is internally motivated.

- One of the primary benefits of following the path of the Hermit is that you are not attached to having to be confined to one particular corporate environment and you have more autonomy in how you perform your job duties.

- The challenges of following the path of the Hermit are the increased necessity of being reliable, the need to be excessively organized about seeking out upcoming assignments and juggling the business matters of being your own boss since it is similar to running your own business with you being the only employee.

Chapter Six

The Path of the Magician

An idea can turn to dust or magic,
depending on the talent that rubs against it.
—William Bernbach

Signpost: The path of the Magician has elements of all the other paths in that it is for a black employee who is independent and free thinking with a creative approach. Where it is different and yet essentially the same is that the path is even more unconventional than the other paths because it addresses the individuals who take a significant departure from a high status job to leave Corporate America.

How Is the Path of the Magician Different Than Any Other Route Out of Corporate America?

A black traveler going down the path of the Magician takes a route both delightful and magical as the name implies but also extremely difficult because it can often be a trip not only without a map but without identifiable destinations.

What does it mean to take the path of the Magician? It's when you do something completely out of the norm of what people consider Corporate America. Taking it a step further, one could argue it's when you take a step that's generally unconventional for a black person, Corporate America aside. It's when you leave the safe, comfortable halls of a high status Corporate America job to do something that makes people do that lifting of the eyebrow trick.

One could argue that all the other paths—those of the Emperor, the Artisan and the Hermit—are similar to the path taken by the Magician.

Since I'm the one creating the categories, for me, the distinction between the route of the Magician and those of the other paths is a matter of status.

While all Americans are into status, with a collective buying power of $656 billion as of 2003, I think we black folks have a particular fascination with looking, driving and acting to the highest status we think we can attain. Our top magazines reflect this—look at an issue of Ebony, Essence, Jet and you'll see as many every day people trying to "floss" as you will celebrities and millionaires. From the ghettofabulous to the black elite, we are culturally a people very in to how we look doing whatever we do.

Unfortunately, the findings from a 2003 study that appeared in Developmental Psychology, a journal published by the American Psychological Association, showed that even young black children are quite indoctrinated with the idea of status and that high status is usually attached to jobs and careers that are considered "white." In this study involving first and sixth grade black children, children ascribed higher status to those occupations that were depicted as having all or mostly white workers and no black workers (based on showing them pictures) than to those jobs with no or low numbers of white workers and all or high numbers of black workers. What is particularly sad and telling about this study, is that the findings showed that the black children have this perception even when the jobs were created jobs, solely invented for the study.

Therefore, it is not a leap for me to think that black adults can be particularly attached to not wanting to lose the "high status" that comes from our Corporate America jobs once we obtain them, especially if that status comes with high salary.

Being Bold and Unconventional Marks the Route of the Magician

Boldness is a quality inherent in all black travelers who leave Corporate America—for those following the path of the Magician, boldness is their primary calling card.

I gotta be honest—while I met a ton of fascinating, amazing people who had great stories for this book, one of my favorite is that of Kathryn Finney. As a graduate of Rutgers University and Yale University, Finney was right in the midst of Corporate America working as an epidemiologist and as executive director of a non-profit organization before becoming the Budget Fashionista.

That's right, sistah girl makes a career of shopping.

Instead of being safely secure in the offices of Corporate America seriousness, she is the founder and chief shopping officer of the TBF Group, Inc.—which owns the website www.TheBudgetFashionista.com.

The websites provide fashion advice, shopping tips and sale information. Finney also provides—for a fee—the services of personal shopping, retail consulting, personal styling and a gift finder service.

Finney knows what it is like to have support—her parents encouraged and supported her in being an upstanding member of Corporate America. But when Finney realized that was not for her, those same parents encouraged her as she headed out on the path of the Magician.

"I have always had a love of fashion, I was a born aesthete. I would design complete fall lines for my Barbie and cheaper, bridge lines for my skipper doll," Finney said, "My parents were very supportive of my crazy ideas—even when they had no clue what I was doing.

They just sort of trusted my instincts, which is an unusual situation for parents."

Finney said that she came from the background where "smart" black girls from the Midwest were encouraged to pursue a career with substance—she wasn't encouraged at that point of her life to pursue a career in the fashion industry. So she received her degree in political science at Rutgers and her degree in Epidemiology from Yale University.

"[While in school], I kept my interest in fashion and retail working everywhere from Marshalls to Nordstrom. I would assist my friends who are actors, directors, etc. in building their wardrobe and developing their style. Many of whom encouraged me to start to look for ways to turn my love of fashion and what I do into a business," Finney said.

While running a major non-profit public agency in Philadelphia, Finney quickly realized that the high stressed world of Corporate America doing something she cared about but wasn't driven by was not for her.

Finney started off her work as the "Budget Fashionista" as a part-time endeavor, but by 2004 left her job to work on it full-time and now has a small staff working for her.

"The character and personality traits that have helped me are my intuition, knack for understanding humanity and assertiveness," Finney said. "Also, anyone who decides to leave very successful careers to go out on their own has to be a little crazy and I am not different. It is much easier to stay in that position and get that somewhat guaranteed paycheck, rather than have to struggle to get your next dime."

The Importance of Mentors and Loved Ones

Finney said that she has been able to make her transition, in part, with the tremendous support of her family and friends, including her husband who has helped design her websites. She has also found others to help her get her path off to a good start.

"I have been able to secure mentors—white, black, men and women, because I do not approach them as if I am attacking them or only looking for a hook up. One of my mentors is a rabbi, who is also the head of marketing for a major internet retailer," Finney said. "The financial aspect has been the hardest, because I went from making a very nice mid- to upper six figure salary to nothing."

Finney exemplifies the concept that people can find it doubly shocking when a black woman takes a radical detour from convention and high status.

"There are those who are very surprised to find out that I am African-American because of my name and my credentials—but I take it with a grain of salt," Finney said of how race has affected her path. "It is their issue to deal with—I am quite comfortable being a successful black woman. This surprise comes from both white and black folks, but they quickly recover from their sense of shock once they hear about my ideas and thoughts."

Finney understands that creating your own path is both about passion and power.

"Working in Corporate America as a young person, you must be willing to release ownership of your ideas to the powers that be— many of whom don't always give you credit for your work. This environment did not work for me. I believed if I thought of the idea and developed it, then I owned it and not someone else just because they are in a higher position than me."

In her current life, Finney has embraced what the true power of ownership is about.

Defying Convention By Taking the Path of the Magician

But what makes the path of the Magician stand out more isn't merely that it is unconventional, it's that it defies convention.

I know of a young brother who was on the management track of a retail company. While he wasn't making anywhere close to the mythic six figures, he was doing more than okay financially. More significantly, he had a job title that made his friends, family and strangers nod knowingly as if to say, "Good for you brother, nice solid job."

But years ago, he decided that management in Corporate America wasn't for him. So now what does my happily married father in his 30s do for a joyful living? He works in a day spa doing manicures and pedicures all day long and loving it.

Over the years Leonard (real name not used) has gotten all kinds of questions about his chosen vocation. He has gotten the bold-faced assertion that he's gay if he is doing fingers and toes for a living. Bisexual? No. Down low brother? Not even a little bit. After that avenue of inquiry has exhausted itself he gets the opposite set of questions. So, you do this as a way to meet the ladies, right? No. You do dabble in more than the nail polish bottle, right man? Nope. C'mon, no erotic fringe benefits in feeling up on women's feet? No, strictly business.

What does motivate Leonard in part is that he likes to help women and men take care of themselves. It gives him satisfaction to be part of the process of pampering and self-care.

Leonard has found that his level of support has wavered over the years, in part, because of people's comfort level with having a man working over their fingers and toes. For the most part though, people have responded to the love Leonard has for the vocation and that's what keeps him happy and emotionally prosperous.

One of the big distinctions between following the path of the Magician as it compares to the other paths is that you may end up working for Corporate America.

Leonard, as a manicurist, has worked for white-owned day spas in the trendy white neighborhood of the Midwest city he lives in. Leonard found this was a case where whites just seemed to be more receptive to what he does.

Keith's success in the white-owned day spa is in juxtaposition to when he had his own "beauty shop" in the middle of the hood and found himself more subject to the fickle winds of his all-black clientele. However, he hopes to go back to the path of the Emperor again while continuing to enjoy his magical way with the pampering.

It's Not About Fitting In a Nice, Neat Little Box

One of the things I discovered while researching and meeting people for this book is that people don't always fit into the nice, neat little categories I've created. That is one of the reasons why I said at the beginning of the book that it is all about being black travelers—those who create their own maps, routes and destinations for the career happiness they strive to have in their lives.

Stephanie T. Humphrey is one of those people who could have gone in more than one place in this book but is in this chapter because I do think there is something particularly magical about an engineer for one of the largest engineering firms in the country for more than nine years who decides to cut to part-time to do modeling and acting.

One of the reasons why I think of the word magic as it relates to Humphrey's story is because of the serendipity at work in how she even ended up on her path.

"A couple of years ago, a friend of mine asked me to participate in a fashion show she was having. There was a woman there who owns a modeling school/agency and she asked me if I had ever done any professional modeling. I hadn't, but the seed was planted," Humphrey said of an opportunity that changed her life and led to her eventually finding an agent.

"At first, it started out as a cool hobby where I could make a couple extra bucks. But the hobby has turned into something I really enjoy doing, and I'm making more money per hour doing less work and much more fun work."

Humphrey has found that creating this different path for herself has found her tapping into the parts of her personality and talent base that an engineering career can't fulfill by itself.

"I consider myself to be highly motivated. I always like to call myself a 'Type A-minus personality' because I don't consider myself quite a type A, but close," Humphrey said. "I try very hard to excel at everything I do, and this new career path is no different. I think I have a pretty good sense of humor and although I tend to be a perfectionist, I don't really take myself too seriously, which is a key trait to have in the modeling business."

While Humphrey still likes certain aspects of Corporate America, she knows that life as an engineer in a major corporation does not present the most creative opportunities for her.

"I love interacting with people and having a job where I'm doing something different every time I work. Also, I'm really just a big ol' ham and I love to have my picture taken," Humphrey said.

Like many black travelers trying to create their own paths, she has found the financial aspect of it the hardest hurdle.

"I'm definitely not in a position to 'quit my day job' just yet due to the erratic nature of the modeling/acting business. I am also still relatively new to the whole thing, and I'm still trying to figure out the best path to take, and learn more of the ins and outs of the actual business," Humphrey said. "My schedule at my full-time job is very flexible but I'd still like to have more time to devote to the pursuit of my other interests."

In the acting world, Humphrey has already discovered that her race can make the door to opportunity seem more like a small crack than a wide open entryway.

"Obviously, there is more work out there for Caucasian models and actors than for Black models and actors. Just ask any black actor in Hollywood. I have personally been to auditions for the 'sassy' black girl, the receptionist, etc. and I think that's always going to be an issue," Humphrey said of the opportunities available. "There are still a lot of prejudices and misconceptions about the way people expect me to conduct myself. I've gotten actual shock and amazement from some white people because I was on time for a booking and could actually read the teleprompter and articulate the words correctly."

But while Humphrey has a high degree of built in respect and status from being an engineer, her boat floats from pursuing her modeling and acting.

Undergoing the Transition In Status

Before I delve into the qualities that make up one taking the path of the Magician, I have to reiterate that in some ways taking on the path of the Magician can best be thought of as the black traveler who decides to joyfully make a transition in status.

For example, a woman who works as a cleaning lady and saves her money to take her hardworking self to medical school where she then becomes a doctor is not following the path of the Magician. However, a doctor who decides to quit the practice of medicine to buy and run a house cleaning service is. What's the difference between making a transition from cleaning to sewing up stitches versus going from writing prescriptions to wringing out dirty towels? Easy. It's status.

The United States of America may not have a formal caste system like India or a monarch complete with kings and queens to keep track, but we Americans of all hues live and die from issues of class and status. Hell, we black folks have *Jet Magazine*— a weekly little magazine (found in beauty and barber shops coast to coast) devoted to our own black royalty.

Not only are black Americans no less subject to judging by so-called classifications, I'd argue we can be guiltier of it than white Americans. Whether we're exhibiting snobbery by figuring out your membership status in Links or Jack and Jill membership or by your membership in the gangs of Crips or Blood, it all ends up being the same game with the differences tied to zip code and wealth.

Therefore, a move up the ladder is what we Americans are supposed to do. Worse, for black Americans, it is what we're made to feel obligated to do. There are not too many of us who have not had thrown in our face (just when we're about to buck expectation and convention) all the black folks who lived and died to create our opportunities of today. More, more, more. More prestige, more money, more status. More.

We blacks especially are not supposed to even dare to take one step down voluntarily. And, of course, anything not up, is down.

I do know of an attorney who actually quit the practice of law, working for a prestigious, lucrative law firm to buy a small house cleaning business. As with most small businesses specializing in a particular service, he was occasionally expected to get his hands dirty too. So, he had a business that required him to actually clean homes himself when a crew member didn't show up.

This lawyer was white. And according to him, his family thought he was crazy. Most likely if he had been black, his family might have had him actually committed to a mental institution.

The point here is that taking on the path of the Magician is the biggest leap of faith of all the paths for a black traveler.

Unfortunately for the person who follows the path of the Magician your motivation may not fall in neat, tight little boxes like those who follow the other paths. The person who follows the path of the Emperor has power and/or control as her underlying motivation, one who follows the path of the Artisan is truly moved by the love of their art and one following the path of the Hermit cherishes independence above all else.

People understand those motivations. They understand them in large part because there are role models for them. While it may be a reach to be a Berry Gordy or a Terry McMillian or an Oprah Winfrey (the ultimate independent contractor in some respects), there is at least a blue print for it.

One can argue that even reaching to attain those things is still in its own way a move up the ladder of American success.

But one following the path of the Magician doesn't often have these nice, neat little edges and role models to fall back on.

Something edgy, less defined usually pushes forward the persons who follow the path of the Magician. And edgy can either be viewed as dangerous or courageous depending on what your own world view tells you about risks.

One of the qualities that are most likely to be seen in a black traveler who decides to pursue the path of the Magician is a spirited audacity.

You've got to dare to view the world as a place in which you will place your square peg firmly in a round hole and that's just that.

Sometimes that audacity is demonstrated by your failure to continue doing what you've always done. For example, a black woman leaving Corporate America to stay home with her kids isn't something seen as commonly in the black community as in the white community. It's not that no black woman has ever been a stay-at-home mother while a spouse works. Rather, that it is not the norm we're raised to seriously view as an option compared to many white women.

Therefore, while staying home to raise your kids isn't a literal form of livelihood, it is a path out of Corporate America that can raise some eyebrows for a black woman who chooses to leave her career to pursue that path.

A Unique Sense of Vision

Another quality that one who follows the path of the Magician may have is the ability to have a sense of vision. By that I mean, you must be a black traveler who has the ability to look at a possible opportunity and envision whether that is something that can truly make you happy and satisfied in the short and the long run. It may be that in following the path of the Magician, you don't start off knowing that you want to do something in particular but an opportunity to do something unusual just presents itself and before you know it, you're caught up in the rapture of a whole new world.

All across the country you see black folks in unusual jobs and you wonder to yourself how that happened. Sometimes people just stumble into unusual jobs and are delighted to find that they love the job. Others find themselves attracted to something odd or unconventional and move heaven and earth to get the position.

One suggestion for a black traveler following the path of the Magician is to seek out, however hard it may be to do so, a mentor. While the mentor can be another black person, please don't limit yourself to finding someone who you are compatible with—find a person who can give you guidance on following your path and support when problems crop up.

Not everyone defines themselves by color and race and looks to limit you because of yours. So look to people who carry the spirit and lives the lifestyle that propels you forward.

Yirser Ra Hotep, formerly Elvrid Lawrence, certainly started out on a very conventional path. Previously, he was a social worker and administrator in the child welfare system of Illinois. At this point, Hotep has followed the path of the Magician and has his own yoga studio in Chicago. In addition to being a yoga instructor, he is a stress management and wellness consultant, writer and teacher.

For Hotep, his path was determined by his sense of internal motivation that drove him to wanting to help others hone theirs.

"I made a commitment to be true to myself and to spend the rest of my life doing things for people from which they would experience internal transformation," Hotep said. "I believed that working in the state system was not allowing me to reach as many people as I wanted and in the ways that I wanted. It was very restrictive and did more harm than good to those we were supposed to be serving."

Because Hotep has studied Kemetic yoga for over 20 years, he felt as if his path in part was already laid down for him by a higher power.

"I felt it was a contradiction for me to work in the environment in which I worked," Hotep said. "It was my faith in the Creator, my ancestral spirits and myself that allowed me to step away from a good paying job with benefits and into the unknown."

After years of working in Corporate America through the government system, Hotep, as many black travelers do, realized that he does not have the personality to work for someone else.

"I can work in partnership with others but not under them. I truly believe that each person has a purpose in life they are supposed to fulfill," Hotep said. "I believe that mine is to share partnership with others but not under them. I believe that [my purpose] is to share knowledge of how to achieve health and well being."

Hotep believes that stepping on the path he has created for himself has naturally enhanced the qualities he needs to succeed.

"Meditation and my training in yoga have enhanced my natural ability to stay focused and single-minded. I also have the ability to visualize what I want and to believe that it will manifest as long as I put the hard work in that I do," Hotep said.

The quality of being a risk taker is an important aspect of taking on any of these paths, but particularly the path of the Magician. Hotep knows that well, saying that one of his strengths is being able to tolerate a lot of uncertainty.

"Even at times when I don't have money I know that the Creator and my ancestors will provide that which I need. This has been proved to me by experience," Hotep said, noting that he supplements the gifts he is given by doing his share of hard work and staying on task. "These are traits that anybody who wants to be free and independent needs to have."

Like many of those who follow the path of the Magician, Hotep has found the two areas where support has wavered have been from the emotional support of family and from the erratic income of doing something that is out of the box. Hotep knows that his family loves and supports him, they just don't always understand what he has created for himself.

"Now that I am doing what I do as a profession, I am asked by my relatives, 'when are you going to get a job?' They don't understand that overall I make more money doing what I do than I ever made working for someone else. The problem is that I am not getting paid every two weeks," Hotep said.

While all black travelers who leave or avoid Corporate America have their share of stressors, Hotep finds himself experiencing obstacles as unconventional as his path. Hotep, for example, has discovered resistance in getting blacks to support his yoga studio from a health standpoint and because many mistakenly assume that practicing yoga as a form of exercise violates their religious beliefs and practices.

Also, like all black travelers, steady finances are always a problem.

"Most people are surprised to see a black man as a yoga instructor. Because of the fact that I try to get corporate clients for my stress management consulting business, the fact that I am black probably limits my access to certain clients or closes the door on possibilities," Hotep said.

Hotep views his time in the government as definitely a long education into the world of Corporate America.

"I consider my 13 years working for the state [of Illinois] as being part of Corporate America in the sense that it was a large multi-billion dollar institution that had tremendous influence in the lives of many people. It also seeks to have its members conform to its values and codes of behavior," Hotep said, saying that he is content to do contract work with Corporate America, including various governmental entities.

When weighing all the pros and cons of embarking on the path of the Magician, Hotep wouldn't take any other walk.

"It's the difference between slavery and freedom," Hotep says. "I work longer hours and endure more obstacles financially at times, but I love what I do and enjoy life to the fullest. I am proud of myself for making the separation and having the fortitude to stick it out. I see my clients and students making tremendous change in their lives in terms of improved health and well being."

Hotep sums up his life as being about seeing the rewards of his efforts.

Those who follow the path of the Magician, as well as the other paths, have found that sometimes the reward is in the journey.

- Following the path of the Magician is about taking a departure from Corporate America into an unconventional job.

- The path differs from the other paths in this book in that it is about taking a shift in status, usually from something socially acceptable to something that seems unconventional.

The path of the Magician often requires a black employee who leaves to have a sense of vision about their life and how it will change and to have the ability to stand strong when they meet resistance on their choices.

Chapter Seven

Transitioning From Safe to Potentially Sorry

He who would fly one day must first learn to stand and walk and run and climb and dance: one cannot fly into flying.
—Friedrich Nietzsche

Signpost: This chapter helps guide black employees who are still in Corporate America but are attempting to put one foot squarely on the path that they've chosen for themselves. It gives tips on what concrete and not so concrete resources a black traveler needs to assemble.

Gathering Your Map, Walking Stick and Water Bottle for the Journey Ahead

In the novel *The Divine Secrets of the Ya-Ya Sisterhood*, by Rebecca Wells, one of the characters says a line I love and find particularly appropriate here, "Life is short but it's wide."

To be a black traveler who tackles taking on an unconventional way of moving through the world, you need to be well equipped.

So, regardless of what path you decide to follow, you have to start with a map. This chapter is about drawing up your own individualized map that can help guide you in your decision and choices.

The Importance of Writing Down Your Plans, Wishes and Dreams

Writing your plans in a private journal would be the place I would recommend to start. A journal doesn't have to be anything formal like something leather bound or with fancy stitching. It can be a 79 cents notebook. All it is has to do is provide you with plenty of space to write, be respected as private by others who may share your personal space and be something that will not be mistaken for something else. More importantly, keeping your journal to draw the map for your journal has to be something you take seriously.

Taking the time to set down and start a journal may seem silly to you. But it's a small step toward focus and commitment. And trust me, if you can't do that, if you can't sit down with even one piece of paper and outline what you want and how you're going to get it, you'll find it only gets harder from there.

The purpose of the journal is to give you a mental starting point of how you get your plan together for your new path. If you stick to just making plans and decisions in your head, you're liable to not think of something and to approach your future in a fuzzy and haphazard fashion.

Henriette Anne Klauser, author of the book *Write It Down, Make It Happen*, quotes the famous line from the 1989 movie "Field of Dreams"—"If you build it, they will come." Klauser views writing your plans down in the same vein by saying, "Building it before he gets there is stepping out in faith, just as writing it down says you believe that it's attainable."

The first thing you should do is try to define exactly what you want to do and add details to it—where you want to live, how much you want to make, what you passionately want to achieve.

Then you need to list what concrete issues stand between you and getting what you need to achieve it. Is it an individual or a group of individuals, like say your family? Is it money, either having start up cash or needing the money you make from the job you have now? Is it a credential or a degree you lack? Is it being too committed or too enmeshed in the job or profession you're currently in?

Now comes the really tough part. Ask yourself, what are the internal obstacles that stand between you and getting to the path you want? That will be a much harder list to create because we often aren't aware of the subconscious thought patterns that hold us back. What's worse is when we acknowledge them but then disguise them as "facts". The things we tell ourselves like, "Black people don't do that" or "I'll starve if I try to do that" or "You've got to know someone to do that" or "I'm not talented or smart enough to try that."

After you've explored every external and internal obstacle you can think of, then you need to ask yourself some more questions to leap frog off of what you've already come up with.

What Questions Do You Need to Ask Yourself?

In the book *Awaken the Giant Within*, motivational speaker Anthony Robbins talks about how asking the self questions is really what thinking is all about.

"Questions set off a processional effect that has an impact beyond our imaginations. Questioning our limitations is what tears down the walls in life," according to Robbins in the book.

I completely agree with Robbins' premise that the right questions put your focus in the direction you want to go and that the mind inevitably comes up with answers. So, asking yourself "Where can I find the money to start my business?" automatically gets you more helpful answers than the question, "What's the point in starting my own business since I don't have any money?"

Both are sentences that end with a question mark but one starts from a place of empowerment and faith while the other sets you up for a downward spiral of doubt.

Therefore, ask yourself, and then write down the answers, what you would need to eliminate your obstacles if you had unlimited resources. The point isn't to focus on how you're going to get what you need, it's just to focus on what you need. By that I mean, it is similar to how you approach baking a cake. If you sit down and say to yourself, I need flour, but I don't have any flour so let me go run to the store and buy some flour—then you've burnt up a lot of time and energy when you get home and realize you don't have sugar, eggs or any of the other ingredients you need for the cake.

That's why you make the list first—so that you can check off what you have, circle what you don't have and plan where you'll go to get your ingredients, especially if you need to go to more than one place. In other words, unless you regularly bake cakes and you always have all ingredients on hand, you're going to need not just a recipe but a shopping list to bake your cake. And what is key to remember is that a recipe and a shopping list are not the same thing. One without the other will leave you remaining hungry for cake.

Now, one of the problems of embarking on a new path, any new path, is that you can often be ignorant of just what it is you don't know but that which you need to know. It's like driving down a road to get to the post office to mail an urgent letter—if there's a big sink hole between you and the grocery store, you won't make it. It doesn't matter if you have the address and you're taking the most direct route, if someone hasn't told you about the sinkhole large enough to swallow up your car, neither you nor your car will make it to the post office.

Sometimes you're doomed to just encounter the sinkhole because it happened just a few minutes before you turned to drive down that street. But sometimes just doing the most minimal research would save you the time that the trouble will end up costing you.

For example, if you're going to quit your job as a stockbroker to go manage a restaurant you might want to do more than just look in the want ads for an open position. You might want to find a restaurant manager or owner to talk to about the benefits and pitfalls of the position, about the pay, about the behind-the-scene tasks required and how one goes about getting one of these jobs without experience.

Don't Be Afraid to Brainstorm

As corny as it may sound, the other way to use your journal is to brainstorm your goals for yourself over the course of the immediate future, the semi-distant future or a lifetime. For example, in the restaurant managing example, do you want to be a restaurant manager as a vocation or is it step to another goal, such as owning a restaurant?

Whatever you write down, don't be afraid to be personal with yourself and go deep. And remember that it's your journal so you may scare yourself with your ambitions and end up sticking the journal in a drawer while you continue life as you know it. But that journal, the blueprint of your dreams, will haunt and taunt you once you write it down. Take my word on that. You may not look at that journal for 10 more years, but the day you pick it up again will be the day you decide to build "it" and see what comes.

The other reason why having a journal handy is an important tool in planning your new career path—if you don't end up throwing the journal in a drawer—is that your plans will require research and you'll need the notes from the research you gather.

Research, Research, Research—Starting With the Information

One of the easiest places to begin your research is the Internet. It's not a perfect tool and it is certainly not the only research tool you should rely on, but in terms of giving you the largest amount of information in the shortest amount of time, it is a great start.

If you don't have access to a computer in your home, you should call your local public library and figure out the policy that allows you to use a computer for free. And if you don't have any computer skills, taking a free or inexpensive computer class might be the first step you take toward furthering your goal. Even if you plan to follow the path of the Artisan, having access to the Internet and having an email address can only benefit you.

After you've narrowed down your goals and have done some basic research on how to pursue your path, the next task for you to conquer will be how to figure out how to tackle what stands between you and starting on your path. In other words, you've got the recipe, now you need to assemble the shopping list.

The Importance of Budgeting

I'll be the first to admit that budgeting or anything related to the concept has never been my strong suit. However, I'll also be the first to admit that lack of budgeting has usually been my chief roadblock to success in just about every significant accomplishment I've attempted.

When you are trying to transition yourself out of Corporate America, the healthiest, most productive time to tackle the budget you need for getting out of Corporate America is while you still have a traditional job.

For example, if I had a dime for every dollar I made in all my years of working while making a steady paycheck, I'd have a dime from every dollar I made that I could be using to smooth out my path now.

The following are the categories typically listed in figuring out what you need to survive: mortgage or rent, each utility bill (including cable or satellite television and telephone), car payments or leases, home repairs and/or maintenance, gasoline for car, car repair and maintenance, transportation costs other than car, child care, insurance (home, auto and any additional), groceries, toiletries, household expenses, clothing and cleaning for clothing, eating out, entertainment and recreation, hobbies, club dues (such as gym or private organizations) gifts or donations such as tithes, healthcare, magazine and newspaper subscriptions, credit card expenses, taxes, pets and miscellaneous expenses.

Totaling that amount and reducing it to a monthly number will help you decide the minimum amount of money you'll need. It also helps you to take a cold look at what can be reduced or cut out entirely.

Another thing to budget in your journal is to realistically set down and write down how you allocate time in your average week. This is important because it is true that time is money—four to six hours a week, for example, watching sports or movies on tape could be spent starting a business, building a body of art work, taking classes, moonlighting or doing whatever jumpstarts your passion.

Even obligations in your life that you are made to feel "have" to be done by you—multiple church activities, community work, disproportionate responsibility for housework or child care—can be reconsidered for purposes of pursuing your path.

In addition to your personal budget, depending on what path you are choosing to embark on, you need to also list any expenses that come associated with that choice. For example, in starting your own business, you may need to consider the following: rental space for the business if it can not be operated out of your home, salaries to employees if someone more than yourself needs to be paid, insurance, supplies, money for an accountant, money for a lawyer, fees for licenses and permits, taxes, etc.

The importance of sitting down to plan a budget can't be skimped on. It's like forgetting to consider concrete when building a sidewalk.

Do You Need to Stop at the Schoolhouse While Traveling Down Your Path?

Depending on what you want to do, the first hurdle you may need to overcome could be as basic as obtaining some sort of degree or certification. If you're leaving Corporate America to do something unconventional, chances are you won't need another college degree if you already have one. But depending on your individual circumstances, that might be a wise choice to make.

The good thing is that a diversity of ways to pursue more education exist besides the traditional full-time college route. There are night schools, accelerated programs, long distance schools and online schools.

For example, if you have determined in your heart of hearts that you desire to be an artist and create works of art that would make Rembrandt weep, then as good as your natural talent may be, going to an art institute or pursuing a degree in Fine Arts from a college may expand and sharpen your talent. Additionally, an institute or a college provides a natural place to make contacts, find out about opportunities, meet colleagues, develop mentors and find other black travelers going down the same path as yourself.

For some, however, getting further education or certification is a necessity. There are certain paths you cannot legally go down unless you're licensed to do so. For example, if you decide to leave your job as a human resources director to become a beautician, in just about every state in the union you will need to have a cosmetology license.

You can't just set up shop and "do hair." While there are people who do that (and most of us black folks have known of at least one bootleg beautician in our day) and manage to stay under the radar, I've found that life is easier when you don't do things that put you in danger of an arrest or a fine.

That is why you can't take one true step forward on your path before you do some basic research because you may not know that you need a certification either legally or practically to go in the direction you want to move in.

Related to the issue of certification or obtaining credentials, part of the research should definitely include seeing whether what you want to do requires membership in a union. If it does not require union membership, you should still investigate whether pursuit of the path would be better furthered by your membership in an organization.

An actress, for example, who wants to break into film, might find her path smoothed somewhat by joining the Screen Actors Guild. In fact, she might find it mandatory to join if she does obtain a role. Since membership in that guild is not cheap, she should add that to her journal as a cost factor.

Transition Is Another Word For Change

If you are in Corporate America and decide to leave it, then you will greet change head on. A study of "change" was conducted by a team of doctors over a 12-year period. "Changing For Good" by Ph.Ds James O. Prochaska, John C. Norcross, and Carlo O. Diclemente explored the six stages of change. Those stages included: pre-contemplation, contemplation, preparation, action, maintenance and termination.

Although the study was conducted more for people trying to break bad habits and/or acquire new ones, I think the stages appropriately apply to black travelers who seek to create a transition from the path out of Corporate America.

The following is how I interpret creating your own career path applying the six stages of change:

The pre-contemplation stage is when you simply go to work every day and don't really give great thought to the other options out there other than working in Corporate America. There might be a little prickle on the edge of the psyche but for the most part you beat it down because it's not comfortable.

The contemplation stage is when some change in your life or someone else's makes you think about the "road not traveled" when it comes to how you make your livelihood. All that may assault your mind is that you know that you don't want to keep on doing what you're doing. You may or may not have given thought to why it is that you do what you do, but you know you want out. In the contemplation stage you may decide that you're just daydreaming.

The preparation stage will find you dealing with the realities of the steps necessary to break free of your safe and secure job in Corporate America. The preparation necessary may still keep your feet planted firmly in your current job but you do find yourself actually taking steps to create the alternate reality of not continuing in Corporate America. For some, that might mean talking to some people who are on the path that attracts you, for others it might mean buying a book on how to start a particular business.

The action stage concretely takes you toward your path. As the word itself implies, you're putting your feet squarely in the direction where you want to go. You may not be completely abandoning your Corporate America position at this point but you've accepted the changes that have to take place in your life for you to move forward on the path of the Emperor, the Artisan, the Hermit or the Magician. At this stage, you will be working either part-time or full-time on your chosen path. The next chapter will address the issues that come with choosing the part-time path.

The fifth stage is called the maintenance stage and this is where you are when you have changed your vision of yourself as being a member of Corporate America. Whether part-time or full-time, you view yourself as firmly on your chosen path and you require the people in your life to make the transition in how they view you also.

The final stage is termination. Since I've adopted the model to fit what I'm writing about I would say that termination is when you've made the final break from Corporate America. As my point has been throughout the book, the issue isn't leaving the business world or government because you hate it. It's the opposite. You leave it because you love something else better. So, when you're in termination stage, you are no longer a formal member of Corporate America, you're living your passion.

Faces of Change

Stephanie Renee, the sistah mentioned earlier who decided not to use her prestigious education in traditional Corporate America, personifies the steps and stages a black traveler covers to get from where they are to where they want to be.

Renee defines herself as an arts administrator, educator, media/ public relations consultant, freelance broadcast producer and copywriter, and a performing artist.

As early as college, Renee suspected she was not cut out for a "nine-to-five suit job" so she started off doing temporary jobs. While doing all this, Renee took heed of her artistic urges and self-published two volumes of poetry while performing in poetry readings in Philadelphia where she lives.

Renee worked in an advertising agency for five years, achieving various promotions but still honoring her love of the written and spoken word (poetry performed publicly).

"After becoming the Senior Account Manager at the [advertising] firm, I realized that I wouldn't be able to grow anymore in that job and it was time to explore a whole new set of skills and career choices," Renee says. "I left the agency in December 1998, incorporated Creator's Child Production in January of 1999 and haven't looked back. I freed my mind and my time to take on employment and begin projects that I was passionate about."

Renee's company Creator's Child Production, has produced spoken word and musical recordings, produced an original musical theatre production, produced commercials and television programs and provided assistance to self-published authors and artists who need management. Renee has started another company, Soul Sanctuary, to separate her educational projects into a non-profit organization.

Renee realized at a young age that she had a love of the arts and of performing. The first career she imagined for herself was to be a broadcast newscaster because it would make her the center of attention, people would value her opinion and she would inform. While she did not take on the broadcasting field, Renee did create a path of her own.

"I think every role I've taken since then had some of those elements [of being a newscaster] in it," Renee says. "I am sucker for knowledge and need to have a profession where learning can be acquired and shared."

Renee credits many influences and internal motivations to giving her the courage to pursue her path.

"My parents trained me to be assertive, competitive and fair. I learned to temper those traits with a healthy dose of creativity in order to make ideas and plans more palatable to various audiences,"

Renee says, who brings her Corporate America experience and skills to the path of the Magician. "Those are the traits I called upon most often in my career in advertising, and what I use now most often in the classroom when working with difficult students. It is creativity—enhanced by a sense of community, intelligence and spiritual growth—that infuses everything I do."

Renee has found one of her most significant obstacles to be societal biases.

"There is a pervasive sense of sexism that exists in all creative careers. Because men still dominate entertainment companies and media/PR firms, women often have to battle the unspoken biases that men hold about how well women can handle the high-pressure, short deadline, multiple task assignments."

Drawing Outside the Lines Can Create an Unsettled Existence

Like just about every other black traveler interviewed for this book, Renee also cites the erratic, if not sometimes non-existent, income that comes with following a path out of traditional Corporate America.

"As a self-employed person, the financial challenges are numerous," Renee says. "[There are] clients who pay late or not at all [and] projects with very flaky objectives that end up costing far more in time and energy than originally anticipated. And it is rare to have the full understanding and support of loved ones because everyone wants to see you have a stable income and job security."

Renee gets through these pressures by having a strong network of female friends in the creative field who mentor each other.

In terms of how being a black has influenced her path, Renee found that having a healthy set of role models from growing up in Washington, D.C. aided her greatly in developing a healthy self esteem. She has also viewed it as an asset in other ways.

"My theatrical experience has greatly benefited from non-traditional casting, allowing me to put a brown face and spin on characters that were not necessarily written for a black actress," Renee says. "I also am very uncompromising about my look. I have had a nose piercing since the early 90s and various natural hair styles for an equal period. This has allowed me to know up front exactly what people think of me and my abilities."

Sticking to principles regarding her appearance, Renee says, has helped her to limit her battles fighting institutional racism.

"My clients know who they're dealing with from the moment I walk in the door. Those with whom I do business accept my cultural heritage and personal choices as a matter of practice."

Renee, who took her Wharton education to create her own path, says all the disadvantages to her path are worth it when stacked up against the joys. The number one benefit is that she chooses the projects that she will work on.

"I do not knowingly take on anything that is a headache or that would force me to compromise my integrity in any way," Renee says. "My schedule is often insane, but I generally have enough flexibility in my time to complete assignments in a manner that works best for my personal biorhythms."

Little things like being able to blast music while working in her home office enhance Renee's enjoyment of her life work. But the biggest advantage for Renee in creating her own path is that she gets to truly honor what brings her passion.

"I am in a position to be my best creative self at all times. In my work, I am consistently using my talents to positively enhance the lives of others. That's a blessing," Renee says.

- Transitioning out of Corporate America is primarily about figuring out where you are and where you're going.

■ One of the first recommended steps is using a journal to spill your goals, ideas, plans and tidbits of stray thoughts about how to get firmly on your path.

■ Doing a budget of your lifestyle is one of the concrete things you can put in your journal—an outline of exactly how much it costs to live the lifestyle you live now so you can know the minimum income you need to generate. Also, creating a budget of your time is important to determine what priorities can be restructured.

■ Some paths require you to take the detour of going back to school—either for a few months to get a certification or for a few years to get a degree of some sort. Regardless, taking the opportunity to learn will expend not just your base of knowledge but your number of helpful personal contacts.

Ultimately, this chapter is about nudging you to remember that transition is just another word for change and that there are a lot of stages in deciding to make a change—stages that don't have to be done all at once.

Chapter Eight

Part-time Path

Problems arise in that one has to find a balance between
what people need from you and what you need for yourself.
—Jessye Norman

Signpost: For many black travelers, the road out of Corporate America isn't one single leap into a new life, but taking on your new path in a part-time capacity if that turns out to be best for you personally and financially. Some handle it by cutting to part-time status on their Corporate America job, others by moonlighting in addition to their Corporate America job.

Holding Down a 9-to-5 While Creating Your Path 5-to-9

This chapter deals with the issue most familiar to those who contemplate leaving the seemingly safe and simple world of Corporate America.

If you're never entered Corporate America in the first place—you started your own business or took over a family business or you pursued your art right out of school or you knew from an early age that the untraditional life was not for you—then this chapter won't make much sense to you.

The bottom line is that money and financial security have a powerful hold on how we live our lives.

While I'm a believer in the importance of having as many options as you can in the world, sometimes those options can hold us prisoner. One of the biggest options we have to take advantage of is education—specifically, degrees, advanced degrees and professional degrees.

Those degrees can open a lot of doors. However, people who don't have the degrees can seem to be the first people irate when you decide not to use it or not use it in a traditional way.

As someone who has a law degree and practiced law for eight years, its amazing how many people who aren't lawyers or who don't have law degrees were downright offended that I stopped practicing law. Recently, I had a telephone conversation with a student loan representative who was particularly indignant with me while talking about a change to processing my loan, "How could you stop practicing law? All those years of school, all that money you spent, all those tests?" She was taken back when my response was, "So what?" She indignantly asked how I could say that. I said that it was just a profession, a job really. I also pointed out (not that it was any of her business) that since I put myself through college and law school it was my money and degrees to spend any way I wanted. People quit endeavors all the time. Would you tell someone to stay in an awful marriage just because they had 'invested" eight years in being married?' I assume the representative must have been divorced because that point she understood.

The Emotional Tie to Being Part of Corporate America

What do degrees and student loans have to do with taking a part-time path out of Corporate America?

Because the emotional investment you may have in what you're doing now as a member of Corporate America may in large part be because of the time you feel you've put into whatever position you currently have.

Many times the part-time option may be one of necessity and I'll get to that in a minute. But sometimes the part-time option is based on you wanting to look as if you're not giving up what you've already worked so hard for. Or as an African proverb says, only a fool tests the depth of the water with both feet.

Not wanting to let go of the branch you're holding on to before swinging on to another branch requires you to sit down with yourself and do some psychological sandblasting. It requires similar analysis to those addressed at the beginning of the book where I talked about asking yourself whether you are copping out or opting out of corporate America.

Stephanie Humphrey, the engineer who is a part-time model and actress, says that one of her ways of handling her path while still maintaining her footing in Corporate America was to deal directly and honestly.

"I've always been very upfront with my manager at my corporate job about my other pursuits and one of the things we agreed on early in this whole dual-career endeavor was that my loyalty, for now, was going to be to that [engineering] job," Humphrey says. "For the time being, I realized that I still had to eat, still had bills to pay, and still needed those benefits, so if it ever came down to it, the corporate job would have to take precedence."

Staying at her corporate job while only able to be on her path part time has come at a cost, Humphrey says.

"That manifested itself in a hugely disappointing way on one occasion when I had to turn down a very lucrative modeling job to meet a deadline. The modeling job would have taken me out of town for five days and it just wouldn't have been possible for me to meet my deadline at work if I had taken it," says Humphrey, saying that it was particularly disappointing because it was a job she didn't have to audition for.

"Another example of the difficulty juggling both is that I currently do modeling work for the QVC Channel. Everything broadcast on the channel is live, so when I was offered the job, I asked that when they book me for shows that the first choice be overnight shows," Humphrey said. "I guess I should have been careful what I wished for because they certainly took my words to heart! "I'm usually on around 2 or 3 a.m. The way I work it out is that if my show gets finished at 3 a.m. or later, I'll go straight to my other [engineer] job. If it ends at 2 a.m. or earlier, I'll go home and sleep and go into work in the late morning."

Humphrey had to make dramatic changes to her life to keep one foot in Corporate America and to pursue her path whole-heartedly. Her adjustments have included working in her engineering job only three days a week. Another adjustment, one more subtle, is that she finds that people take her part-time vocation more seriously.

"When I first started, it was kinda just something I was doing 'on the side' for fun mostly," Humphrey says. "I love it, and I've made the decision to pursue it seriously, and I believe my manager realizes and respects that. The only sacrifice I feel I've had to make is in the type of work I now get at my corporate job. Sometimes I think I'm not being given the responsibility I could be getting because they know that I'm not available full-time and that my interests [now] lie elsewhere."

Humphrey recognizes that this is the price she pays for pursuing her career in modeling and acting while still holding on to her lucrative and prestigious career as an engineer. Humphrey recognizes that for all the inconveniences of her dual life, the stability of a weekly paycheck has cushioned the bumps of following her path. At least for now.

As examples like Humphrey show, how you decide to approach the part-time path determines whether you are copping out or opting out.

Keeping Your Full-Time Job in Corporate America

First of all, there are two basic but different things I mean when I address working part-time in Corporate America. One is the obvious one of choosing to work fewer hours at your Corporate America job and officially going to part-time status.

The other way to pursue your path part-time is not really part-time, it's more like pursuing your dream in your spare time. In other words, you continue to work full-time in your Corporate America job but you pursue your path when you're not scheduled to work. I know of a postal delivery carrier (a mailman) in his 40s who has spent the better part of his adult life delivering the mail by rain, sleet and snow. He and his wife have raised a couple of kids off his salary and are helping to raise a couple of grandchildren. But my man Rick (not his real name) managed to use some of his "spare" time in the last few years to produce a jazz album on which he plays all the instruments.

Rick more than once thought about abandoning his life with the U.S. Postal Service to pursue his music fulltime. But he knew he wasn't ready or willing to commit to the wholesale upheaval of his life. However, he still carried out his dream step by step. Is Rick making any significant money from selling his CD or does he think he might ever be able to do this as a fulltime endeavor? No, he doesn't plan on going the full-time route as a musician, no matter how good his music is and how much work as he has put into it. He has a vision of the priorities of his life, which includes his family, and knows he doesn't want to completely walk away from the security of his job.

In part, it's because he lives in the Midwest, and he didn't see uprooting his life and re-shifting his priorities to another place and to another way of life. Yes, he loves his music. But at this stage of his life, he loves time and space with his family more. He's at peace.

On the other hand, another brother I know has also pursued his music in his spare time. He is a computer technician working for a large corporate conglomerate. Benny has even gone as far as building a music studio in the basement of his house. Like Rick, Benny has produced musical albums, and in part has done so because he doesn't have wife and children to compete for his time. However, unlike Rick, Benny would like to abandon life as he knows it and pursue his path fulltime.

However, while the two brothers from another mother have done similar things—worked full-time jobs while pursuing their paths—one is happy with the way he has chosen to have the music in his life, while the other is afraid to strike out on his path.

I use the word afraid very deliberately. Some would argue that Benny is being smart, playing it safe, acting maturely. Why? Because he's staying year after year in a job he hates. And some people, hell, a lot of people, feel that a hated but regular paycheck is better than irregular money doing something you love.

Sometimes the safe, stable approach is the way to go. Sometimes it's just chicken. What makes the difference is whether there is any plan to your path, any purpose in your pursuit.

Joel Brown is an in-house attorney for a Fortune 500 company's legal department. He supplements his life with poetry. Or as Brown puts it, "Before law school, there was poetry."

Brown, however, understands that the practicality of making a living doesn't crowd out pursuing the passions of your heart.

"After I started working for a [law] firm, I realized that being a lawyer was not the truest expression of my spirit. I like being a lawyer—the academic exercise, the mental gymnastics—but the profession is very inhumane," Brown says. "When I clerked for firms while I was in law school, I had friends as well as colleagues (including partners in the firm) tell me that although they thought I would make a good lawyer, that perhaps my passion lay elsewhere. I remember vividly working for a big firm in Minneapolis and making a top-dollar salary, but absolutely dreading getting out of bed every morning."

Brown said he was fortunate to learn early in his legal experience that it was not something he planned to do until the grave.

"I marvel at how attorneys can work in the profession for ten plus years. I can't see myself doing that. The cost would be too high emotionally," Brown says. "A lot of people stay in the profession because they have a lifestyle to maintain; i.e. a mortgage to pay, kids to feed, a spouse to placate. Fortunately, I have enough freedom when lawyering is not a need, per se. I love the law, but there will be a time when the law will no longer take center stage. I imagine that time will come sooner rather than later."

Despite his fulltime living as an attorney, Brown identifies himself as a writer when people ask him what he does for a living. As a gay black male, he uses his poetry as a form of expressing to the world the diversity of lives and spirit.

"I saw poetry as a way to feed my spirit, and to balance the sometimes insane world of the legal profession. A lot of people think that poetry and law are incongruent," Brown said. "But in each vocation, I am manipulating language. The two are not all that different at all at the core, except that poetry is very celebratory, and law can be very adversarial."

In following the path of the Artisan, albeit, a part-time path, Brown hopes to one day make his poetry a full-time vocation, including the publishing of his books of poetry. Currently he publicly performs his poetry at various civic, spiritual and artistic events.

Brown views his poetry as a full-time vocation that accompanies his full-time job as a lawyer.

"I always make time to write. Fortunately, I don't work long hours at work, so I am able to spend at least two hours a night writing when the mood strikes me," Brown says. "However, on those occasions when I stay up late writing, it makes for an interesting if not exhausting morning at work."

Brown admits that sometimes when the poetic muse strikes while he is busy being a lawyer, he doesn't just put it off until he has spare time, an admitted luxury for the job he does.

"There have been occasions where I have deferred work in order to complete a thought, an idea or some form of creative expression," Brown says. "Mind you, I am highly respected in my office and have been promoted several times, so the writing has not compromised my work. But there are definitely times when I would rather be writing instead of reviewing legal cases and briefs or talking with opposing counsel. This is a balancing act that I have to approach delicately."

I've mentioned keeping a journal for purposes of setting out on your path. Keeping the journal is a way to contain your goals and make them concrete. On the other hand, the plan isn't always linear. Sometimes you have to take a couple of steps back to make real progress.

Taking Baby Steps on Your Path

Sometimes you have to make a small tentative step now to prepare yourself for the big leap in the future.

At the beginning of my legal career, deep in my heart I knew I wanted to write. So in my spare time I wrote a novel. I went to a writers' group every weekend where we critiqued each other's work, I traveled to out-of-town writers conferences; I bought books about writing books. I pursued my love of writing part-time because I was in no way ready to give up the career I just started. However, I knew a year into practicing law that it wasn't for me. But I wasn't going to just walk away after a year or two. I wasn't ready to give up the money or the status. More pointedly I was not willing to face the prospect of looking like a big old loser to the world to give up the exalted legal profession so soon.

A few years later, when the urge to still write burned up the blood in my veins, I took the approach of going part-time in the technical sense—I cut back on my hours. Well, in the legal profession, as with many others, that can be career suicide. You're not viewed as taking your career as seriously. And truth be told, I wasn't. As is, continuing even part-time as lawyer felt miserable. I just didn't want to do it at all.

And after eight years, I stopped. Cold turkey. Financially it was damn near a complete disaster but I think I saved my own life by making that choice. For me, even part-time Corporate America was a cop out because I was miserable on the inside and really only found joy in writing, and public speaking related to my writing.

However, I'll be the first to admit that earlier in my life the part-time path of doing it in my spare time was actually the perfect route for me. One of the reasons was because I needed time to work on my craft. While I've always believed I had natural talent as a writer, I had a real limited sense of the craft and business of writing. And to the extent that I had tons to learn, frankly, I would prefer doing that on someone else's dime rather than my own. Also, early in my legal career, while I knew I didn't love it, I hadn't come to hate the law yet either. But as the years passed my dissatisfaction increased and the choices I made reflected that dissatisfaction. I picked new jobs as a form of escape.

As a friend and I just recently talked about, it takes far longer to unbury yourself from a bad decision than to make a good decision in the first place. Granted, at the time, sometimes we convince ourselves that a bad decision is really a good decision. But the truth reveals itself in time.

And sometimes taking the part-time path can be a way to determine if a decision you really want to launch has the fuel to get off the ground.

Taking the Spare-Time Path

The spare-time path requires fewer considerations than the true part-time path. For one, to a certain extent, what you do in your spare time is your business anyway and no one expects it to have any more crossover value than an accountant being a weekend gardener.

According to the Department of Labor statistics, in early 2005, 7.7 million Americans, representing about 5.5% of the workforce, held down multiple jobs. Now granted, that statistic goes side by side with the numbers that show black unemployment of 10.6% compared to the country wide unemployment percentage of 5.5%. But for those black travelers who are already firmly entrenched in Corporate America, finding that second job may not prove as daunting—especially if it is in an area or field different from your "regular" job.

However, if the path you are choosing to follow in your spare time is the path of the Emperor—starting your own business—in most cases it's best to keep that to yourself. Some employers have policies out right banning the taking on of second jobs, or at the very least, require you to inform them of the second job. Since each policy is phrased differently with varying parameters, only you can decide how you choose to start on your path will be handled.

And if your part-time business has anything at all to do with your regular Corporate America job you should keep down right silent. Of course, it goes without saying that if pursuit of your spare time job violates a contractual provision of your corporate position you should refrain from pursuing it. In fact, if you have a contract with your employer—and most people don't—then you should probably consult an attorney to make sure there are no provisions that will create a problem. More often than not, the illegal and the unethical eventually catch up with you.

In general, however, my belief is that when it comes to business, it's best to keep your outside endeavors to yourself, otherwise your employer will keep an eye on you because they will question your commitment to work.

Stephanie Humphrey, the engineer who also acts and models, touched on that when she talked about how going to part-time status affects her work assignments because of concern about her priorities.

And unfortunately, unless you work in a department or a workplace where part-time and alternate work schedules are commonplace, concerns about your dedication will be questioned for the time you choose to stay in Corporate America.

Another piece of advice necessary for those who work part-time in Corporate America but pursue their passion in their spare time— taking your work seriously. I know of a woman who has the ability to hate her job dearly but yet go to work everyday with a smile on her face giving 100%. I have never had that ability. As I got older I got better at masking my discontent but I can't honestly say it became undetectable. My friend, on the other hand, had folks at every job she departed dealing with it in jaw-dropping shock once she announced she was walking out the door.

But if you're going to keep working and bringing in the dollar bills the old-fashioned way with a regular paycheck then you have to keep your bottom glued to the bottom line. Otherwise, you're going to be committing an act of unconscious sabotage. By that I mean, doing such half-assed work that you put yourself on the chopping block to get fired or pushed out.

Many people would vociferously deny that they are committing career sabotage. Most people honestly believe they do their best every day when they go to work. The truth is that a lot don't. And it's one thing if you know that and pay the price willingly. It's another when you operate in denial.

Since I began writing this book, a successful black soldier in Corporate America hierarchy was terminated from his job. It just so happens he was pursuing the path of the Artisan in his spare time, which his former employer knew of. Although his part-time artistry was not directly cited as a reason for his dismissal, I believe that based on the reasons given, the employer questioned my friend's devotion to his work.

Additionally, while this black traveler believes he did a great job for his employer, he may have failed to grasp that his part-time passion had a bigger hold on him than he realized and maybe, just maybe that showed in his work.

Therefore, if the desire to walk your path is so strong that you find yourself distracted or lethargic when you're at work, then you need to get to your path quickly. Pull out your journal, look at your plans, plan the work and work the plan. Miserable serves nobody, especially yourself and your family.

Now if you honestly believe you're fulfilling your role in Corporate America with no undue harm to yourself or others, then walking the path of the black traveler may be just the path for you. That is particularly the case if the path you are trying to follow is that of the Artisan.

For one, creating art requires a body of work. Especially if you're looking to one day have the fulltime livelihood of selling it. Even performing artists need to have performances to add to their resumes and their list of credits. And before you can just spring yourself on the world, you need to have something to show.

Sometimes finding time to create art can be easier if your dedication is high and demands force you to find time in your schedule. I wrote two books, one published and one unpublished while working full-time as an attorney. I've found the other two books I've written outside of Corporate America much more difficult to write.

The beauty of working full time, which is the advantage to use when walking your part time path, is that you have to fight for your time. It's like the adage—if you want something done quickly, give it to a busy person.

But time has to be carved out to create the path. Otherwise, you'll just be spinning your wheels dreaming instead of truly laying down the building blocks to build a new and concrete reality.

Choosing to follow the path of making your life in Corporate America nothing more than a part- time job can have some serious pitfalls because one foot is still firmly planted in the life you're trying to leave.

Can Part-time Be Long-Term?

For one, ask yourself how viable this option is for you on in the long term.

Once you decide to cut back on your hours at your job, your dreams are no longer in the closet. You not only are making them a reality but you're announcing to the world, starting with your employer, that you mean business. There is no more flying under the radar once you decide to cut back on your visible presence at work.

Obviously, the first consideration to make is can you financially afford to cut your hours. Many people don't operate on a real budget. We operate with a vague sense of "about" how much money we need to earn to support our lifestyle. If you're going to go to part-time status then you have to make a list of your expenses and do dollar and cents analysis on just exactly how much money you need to add to the personal coffers.

The other thing you have to ask yourself if you decide to go part-time to pursue your passion is what you're willing to give up. If you cut down from a 40 hour a week job to a 30 hours a week then you need to figure out before you go part-time what part of your life is that 25% drop in income going to come from and what will you do with that 10 extra hours a week.

When I decided to go part-time in my job as an attorney (before ultimately quitting altogether) I had to ask myself what "luxuries" I couldn't live without.

I was willing to cut back drastically on travel, new clothes and new furniture for the house. I wasn't willing, however, to cut out lattes from the neighborhood coffee shop, magazines, sushi twice a month or cable television. While everyone has the same baseline necessities of shelter, food and transportation, the variety in which those necessities can be bought are infinite.

Once you've figured out your financial budget, you next have to figure out your time budget. What are you going to do with the extra time? You need to have a concrete plan, otherwise, I guarantee your extra time will not be spent on pursuing the goals on your path. It will be spent on errands, goofing off and on the O.P.P. also known as, Other People's Priorities.

If you are going part-time at your job in Corporate America to start a business, will you spend your extra time providing services, making goods, managing a staff? Or will the extra time be spent having more peace of mind to prepare for your new business?

If you are going part time to pursue art on the path of the Artisan, will you put yourself on a schedule to have more time to paint or draw or write or sculpt? Will you use the extra time for rehearsals or classes?

The black traveler who follows the path of the Hermit is the person who will have the biggest comfort level with going to part-time status. For some black travelers, going part time in Corporate America may end up being a semi-permanent solution. He or she decides that simply being away from the full time pressures and expectations of the rat race makes them breath easier by day and sleep easier at night.

Therefore, the black traveler who follows the path of the Hermit may be the one category of persons that doesn't really need to plan what to do with the extra time. The extra time may itself be the goal.

If you follow the path of the Magician there are an infinite variety of uses extra time from Corporate America may afford you. You may use the time to obtain certification, go back to school or otherwise use the time to get experience doing what you have a passion for.

How do you decide when to make the transition completely out of Corporate America? The two big issues you have to consider in deciding to go part-time are the same general issues you have to consider when deciding whether this option continues to be viable.

Counting Your Pennies and Dimes to See if Your Path Makes Sense

The first is money. Clearly, unless you're independently wealthy or you have an understanding spouse or partner willing to carry the total financial weight of the household, you have to determine if you can afford to leave Corporate America entirely. Feelings and passion aside, it boils down to dollars and cents. Or as someone once said to me, "If it don't make dollars, it don't make sense."

The other overriding issue for someone who is considering whether to make the entire leap from Corporate America to pursuing their path is establishing whether you can mentally make the leap. Even a fractional hold on your position in Corporate America is still a hold. You still get to have the status symbol of saying where you work.

An interim step for you to consider, depending on whether your workplace allows it, is to take an unpaid leave of absence or sabbatical to see if the path you want to walk is really the journey for you.

That option, of course, requires you to deal with the temporary loss of income as well as the stigma that may be attached to your time out if you decide to return to Corporate America.

In the end, whatever transitional approach you take has to be one that makes your life more gratifying. If the stress of your transition causes more unhappiness than the pursuit of your path, it doesn't necessarily mean that the journey needs to be abandoned. It may mean that you need to take a different route.

For someone who is working to build something in their spare time, the stress and toll on the family may require a small reduction in hours from the corporate job.

For the person who has gone to part-time status but isn't bringing in enough money, they may have to go back to fulltime status and devote more of their spare time to pursuing their dreams.

The key point to remember is that creating a future for yourself requires you to be a visionary—you have to constantly assess how to leverage the advantages to get what you want. If you just look at the options that are spelled out in front of you, it will be harder to move forward.

- In deciding that you want to create a new life for yourself out of Corporate America, you may realize that you can't completely walk away.

- From a practical standpoint, you may be required to continue your full-time path in Corporate America because you need the money and/or you need the time to develop a skill, market a client base, make contacts or build a body of work.

- Some handle the need to keep one foot in Corporate America by cutting back to part-time status, others handle it by taking on an additional position or schooling.

It's important not to underestimate the emotional and psychological attachment to being perceived as having a position in Corporate America.

Chapter Nine

Walking Across A Shaky Bridge To Get To Your Path

*Many hands, hearts, and minds generally
contribute to anyone's notable achievements.*
—Walt Disney

Signpost: Part of building a new path out of Corporate America involves having plenty of support—emotional as well as practical. This chapter explores ways to garner support from family and friends, as well as find ways to obtain financial support.

Having Sufficient Guardrails Along the Way

You've done it. At the very least you've decided to do it. Your mind and heart are in synch about what you want and plan to do. You're either going to start that business or pursue that art or be an independent contractor or left the practice of medicine to run off to the circus.

It takes a lot of hard work and internal awareness to get to the point where you're really ready to head out on your path.

But sometimes the hardest thing you can obtain for your path is the external support you need. With the best map in the world and the clearest sense of direction backed with undiluted motivation you won't get far if you have no vehicle, no money to obtain transportation and detractors constantly putting roadblocks in your way.

Everyone's set of roadblocks is different; but they tend to fall under the same general categories.

Family Ties are the First Places to Look for Support

The first and often times the most significant base of support is family.

Even in the most dysfunctional of families, our relatives do mean well and are protective of our well being. At the very least, you know which of those loved ones really have your best interests at heart and which ones are just sticking their nose in your business because they're always hunting for scent.

How you deal with those well meaning family members depends on which of two categories they fall in. One category is those family mentors, such as parents or older relatives who assisted in your upbringing. Those relatives have a lifelong, authentic habit of worrying about you. Therefore, if you still remain close to this particular category of relatives, then depending on individual circumstances, it is usually best only to tell them about your plans when you are completely committed to follow through and you pretty much have set the chain of events in motion. It's also best to keep the information general regardless of how many details exist to share.

Because this kind of resistance is based on love and protectiveness, if you know you have this kind of potential opposition in your life, then you need to be confident and firm in your path before opening your mouth to them. In other words, these are not the folks to process with. By process I mean plan out loud, test out ideas. If you're feeling unsteady or doubting, then they will use sheer will and emotional authority to steer you right back to the Corporate America life.

Cecelia Aderonke, the actress who uprooted herself to move to New York City, didn't tell her mother about the move until a week before she left. Because she knew her mother would worry about her, not only did she not tell her mother, she didn't tell a lot of her friends about her plans.

"I only told three or four people that I thought would absolutely support me," Aderonke said. "It helped to start identifying the eagles from the scorpions, the crabs in the barrel."

If you're blessed to have the kind of parents, in-laws or other important authority figures who will not only support your flight from Corporate America but help you fluff out your wings, then you can tell those relatives earlier and share a few more details.

The point is you need to know what kind of people you have. You only have to look to how they've received, responded and directed you in every other major decision of your life from the time you learned to crawl to predict how they'll take the news of your departure from Corporate America.

What if these folks present vocal, passionate opposition to your plans and are affirmatively trying to steer you away? That's when you have to indulge in a "get real" moment with yourself, away from these influential relatives and remind yourself over and over again that you're grown and it's your decision. It's only when you are able to truly operate as the adult you are—whether you're 21 or 51—that you can honestly expect your parents or former caretakers to respond to you as an adult.

We black people, as a culture, can take the whole "honor thy mother and father" concept to a whole, slightly dysfunctional level. Personally, I think there is a wide difference between honoring them and not disrespecting them and the other extreme of treating them as if they have automatic input on every meaningful aspect of your life until death do you part.

For those people who know that the relatives who oppose them the most stringently are the very folks they'll have to hit up for a loan if the best laid plans turn to manure, you may have to just suck up a little bit more of their discontent. As the saying goes, "the ass you kick today may be the butt you have to kiss tomorrow."

Partners on the Path Can Be Critical

However, another category of loved ones exists also. These are the more non-essential relatives, to be polite. These are kinfolks who you pretty much only see at big family events (reunions, funeral, weddings and hospital vigils) and who haven't contributed concretely to your life since buying you a chocolate Easter bunny when you were in grade school. These are the relatives who you should entertain no discussion with about your plans. I mean zero conversation. In fact, don't even bother telling them because they'll find out anyway. And when they do offer their two cents worth, just respond by answering briefly and moving with a quickness to a conversation that involves something that drips off of their branch of the family tree. "So, I hear you have another grandbaby. Got any pictures?" or "I hear Lamont's out on parole, how's he doing?" Whichever is appropriate.

Family members with who you have an interdependent relationship have a completely different set of issues to address. Societal mores, legal definitions and religious issues aside, I include live-in lovers in this category along with spouses and, in some cases, dependent children.

In other words, anyone who is directly and immediately impacted by your change in financial or even societal status needs to be in the loop the second you even think about taking steps to alter your relationship with Corporate America.

In the 2002 movie "Brown Sugar" with the delightful Taye Diggs and Sanaa Lathan, the married character played by Diggs decides to quit his lucrative, high status job as a music producer with an established recording company to start his own recording company. He had enthusiastically decided to start on the path of the Emperor.

Only problem is, he didn't bother telling his wife that he was thinking of doing all this before giving his walking papers to his employer. The fact that he had made his beautiful female best friend played by Lathan his confidant in all things of importance and their relationship was actually the whole point of the movie.

My illustration is to show that we all know that you just can't do that to your immediate family members. And you "can't" on a couple of levels. One, of course, is money. Often times, your new life brings in less money, at the very least, less reliable money. The conversation in the average person's head is going to go a little bit like this: "If I'm your wife or husband or life partner then I need to have time to decide if I'm willing to take that collective financial hit. It doesn't matter whether I bring in no income, 50% of the income or 80% of the income. And if we have children together that we're raising, you really must be out of your damn mind to think you're going to spring this on me without input or warning."

On another level, if I'm your spouse or housemate I need to have the opportunity to decide if I want to participate in your new lifestyle. In the "Brown Sugar" movie, the wife of Taye's character liked his high status, high profile and glitzy lifestyle. She was a highly paid professional who liked having a husband who contributed to their pretty Buppie image. While some may have considered her priorities superficial, they were her priorities to have and she had the right to decide, or at the very least adjust, to a lifestyle of less money, less glamour and different priorities.

Therefore, I would suggest if you hold your relationship and family in as high regard as you hold the passion for your path, you start the discussions sooner rather than later. In an ideal relationship, your passion for your path won't come as a complete surprise to your beloved. If you've always dreamed of starting your own business, selling flowers or of painting breathtaking Italian landscapes, your significant other should know about this abiding passion before you decide to break free from the shackles of Corporate America and do it.

If he or she doesn't know of your inspirations, well then you may receive opposition from them sufficient to stop your plan dead in its tracks. You may be just as much an adult dealing with your partner as you are dealing with parents, but, unlike with parents, a spouse does have a vote because it affects them daily. That's why the early you discuss your plan, the less opposition they might have later on.

Ultimately, though, if your spouse or partner puts their foot down and makes creating this new path for yourself unbearable, you will have to make a choice. Every situation is unique obviously, but most of the time I don't believe that a black traveler will be required to choose between family and a new career path. Individual circumstances will require you to craft a compromise that everyone can live with.

Your compromise may mean that you have to go the part-time path or the spare time path instead of completely quitting your job. You may have to postpone your plan until the last or first child is out of the nest. You may have to wait out the prior plans of your loved one already set in motion, such as finishing school, getting their own business off the ground or handling family issues.

Whatever you end up doing is a very personal, individual solution that only you can create based on the circumstances you have to weigh. Personally, I was fortunate enough to not have anyone else to consult when I made my major life change to leave Corporate America. At the time, I wished I had the spouse to share it with—to celebrate the highs and lows as well as help ease the financial pangs. But it didn't take long to learn that I might not have made those changes if there was even one other person to consider.

Hopefully, if there is resistance from your immediate family, what I hope you can do is focus them on the ways this can benefit the family or the relationship. It helps to show them that you will be happier following your path rather than continuing to conform for the sake of conformity.

One group of people I think should be included in the support group you create are your children. While on the one hand, I'm not a proponent of a child-centered society where everything revolves around the wants (not needs) of children, I do believe that sharing with them your process and including them in the fruits of your success will provide a long-term positive benefit.

You will be offering yourself up as a role model. You can show them that as a black American you have the same right to create your destiny as any other American. And you can also show them that they have the power to recreate success if their light dims and would grow brighter going in another direction.

Good Friends Provide A Wealth of Support

Another area of emotional support that is critical to cultivate in pursuit of your path are your friends. Often times when you pursue your path with vigor and determination, life reveals who your true friends are.

Friends, like spouses and life partners, are a reflection of who you are and what your life looks like when you meet them. Some of those people will have the maturity, security and inherent capacity to flow with whatever changes you make in your life. One of my closest sistah girlfriends has the amazing ability to know, just from the way I say hello, whether she needs to cry, curse or celebrate with me. Those friends are true treasures to never take for granted.

Other acquaintances and friends aren't quite so sturdy. Like items in a Midwesterner's wardrobe, most of them are not meant to be all season. When change in your life hits, you discover the hard way that some of those friends really can't handle any season.

Deciding to abandon Corporate America will certainly trigger other people's "stuff." I've observed that even people who aren't in traditional Corporate America themselves may act up and be less than supportive when you decide to leave. What happens is that others can sometimes get very invested in you being the lawyer friend or the doctor buddy or my ace who is a stockbroker on Wall Street.

If you're particularly unhappy in your job in Corporate America they might be thrown off center by you actually doing something about your life other than complaining. It's a similar dynamic to one person in a group of friends losing weight or no longer engaging in a regular bad habit. The change causes the running buddies to get uncomfortable. In essence, when you decide to reinvent how you make your livelihood, some will take your seeking a change as a rebuke to their continuing to remain in Corporate America.

The only thing you can really do is to decide which friends deserve reassurance and support so they can in turn support you on your glorious ride and which friends require you to leave them behind at the station.

Cutting off a friendship merely because they fail to support you in a new path may seem harsh. It isn't as if they are necessarily being deliberately and knowingly destructive to your confidence and happiness. Some of those people can be dealt with simply with less or different contact.

Time and success will help things fall into place. Life is never static so as you proceed on your path you will attract new friends and more understanding acquaintances to your life.

Jess Mowry, a writer who has been in Corporate America in various jobs including truck driver, marine engineer and aircraft mechanic, had discovered that people can be very uncomfortable with not being able to figure out what Corporate America box to put you in.

"I've found that calling oneself a writer often brings on a barrage of additional questions as the questioner tries to ascertain that one actually DOES something for a living in the line of real work," Mowry says. "Thanks to my dad, I've always regarded 'real work' as an activity involving shovels and sweat."

Not giving a lot of concern to what others think of him, Mowry says, is one of the keys to how he gives himself internal support, along with other qualities.

"Possessing the ability to be alone for long periods with no one to relate to, as well as having the self-discipline to work alone and get things done. The latter quality is essential for a writer, but also comes in handy for a truck driver, mechanic, or in any other profession where one is mostly unsupervised," Mowry says. "Having the ability to work alone often allows one to define one's own perimeters in a company and make one's own rules.

One of the biggest obstacles that Mowry feels he has faced in carving out the path of the Artisan for himself is that of racism.

"In regard to writing—and not surprisingly—I encounter racism on every level, from simple ignorance to outright hatred. I'm frequently in the position of having white people telling me how black people (my characters) ought to behave and/or speak, and then having to decide whether to stand up for the truth as well as my pride, or hold my tongue and submit for the sake of a project."

One of Mowry's strengths is to look at being black as something to be positively "exploited" to its fullest.

"This begins with the realization that a black person is seldom—if ever—going to be accepted in a predominantly white workplace; and constantly striving for acceptance is generally a big waste of time and energy. Even the most enlightened white folks feel guilty about how black people have been treated throughout most of European history. Normal people resent feeling guilty and usually transfer their resentment onto whatever is causing the guilt," Mowry says. "Far better, I think, to devote one's time and energy toward find a way to become successfully self-employed, or at least carve out an unassailable niche in a corporate environment."

The other huge bridge you often have to cross in changing the direction of your career out of Corporate America is figuring out a way to finance it.

Taking the Leaps of Faith and Looking For Angels

Some paths can't be financed in the direct way—you just have to take a leap of faith and hope it works out. For example, if you decide to quit your job as a television producer to go join the rodeo—follow the path of the Magician—you have limited recourse in making the switch from a higher paying profession to a lesser paid one, regardless of the bigger rewards.

However, for other paths, lack of money shouldn't stand in the way. At the very least, you should investigate all options so that you are making informed decisions.

For example, if you decide that you want to take a path that requires more education than you currently have or a different education than you've obtained you will usually find that many opportunities to obtain money for that exist. The most obvious financing for school and student loans is through the Federal government and through the schools you apply to. You can also ask institutions other than colleges and universities if they provide loans and alternative financing options.

Also, explore if you can get advanced credit for your life experiences. That is a form of saving money since that will shorten the time you need to stay in school.

If you contact the institution to which you are interested in applying, one of your first calls should be to the financial aid office to see if they can put you in the direction of not just loans, but grants and scholarships.

On the subject of scholarships, you shouldn't avoid any dark corners when it comes to researching whether any organization you're even remotely affiliated with offers scholarships. From social organizations to professional organizations, there is always some category you fit in that someone wants to throw money at for the purpose of bettering yourself or giving you a break. The amount of one scholarship may not be a "full ride" sufficient to pay for all your expenses but every little bit can add up to a lot of bits.

If the money you need to set out on your path is to start your own business, then there are several possibilities to be investigated for the purpose of providing loan money to small businesses.

The book couldn't begin to detail the different kinds and sources of loans available to small and minority businesses. However, included in the places to get that information are the following: the U.S. Small Business Administration (SBA), the Minority Business Development Agency which is with the U.S. Department of Commerce, Small Business Development Centers located in every state, state economic development agencies, and the Service Corps of Retired Executives ("SCORE") which is free and confidential.

The bottom line is that there are dozens of programs to look into if you want to seek financing of your business—each city has its own set of programs and people who can help you.

Although this not an exhaustive list, among the common kinds of financing for small businesses are the following: Angel investing for new and smaller businesses, a home equity loan against your house, cash advances against your credit cards and equipment leasing for businesses that require equipment.

The last resort (and I mean dead last) for funds to finance your dream are borrowing from or taking a loan against your retirement savings or regular savings. I know this goes against every good piece of advice you've ever been given about planning for the future and saving for a rainy day. Some would say that it's down right irresponsible to consider it as an option. That's why I characterized it as a last resort, one to only consider when every other option has been tracked down and spit in your face.

If you've been blessed with good jobs and lots of common sense where money is concerned, raiding your savings will not be the same thing as depleting it. But if you're like me, only blessed with one half of the equation, then this approach can leave you in a bind.

However, I'm a believer of the adage do what you love and the money will follow.

Maintaining Your Balance on the Tightrope

In a nutshell, I think the key to walking the path as a black traveler out of Corporate America requires you to maintain a healthy sense of balance at all times. Operating out of desperation or taking an extremist position will almost always find you in a trick bag.

In other words, don't quit your job without thought, think about why you hate it and then plan what you're going to do next. Don't just dream and talk about what you're going to do, put it to paper.

Plan it with as much concreteness as if you were writing a grocery list. Don't look at writing the list as if it's some b.s. flakiness. You'll be writing the story of your life.

Ratana Tshibanda, has been the owner of RT Productions, a fashion event production company, for the past five years.

Tshibanda's stint in Corporate America for about six years was for a major chain of national department stores as a fashion manager and regional director.

Parlaying the expertise she developed in Corporate America helped Tshibanda learn and perfect skills to help her launch her vision.

"I am very creative, detail oriented, have a take charge personality, [am a] perfectionist, and will do what it takes to get the job done (no matter how large or small the task)," Tshibanda says. "I needed to cultivate a career that allowed me to be creatively challenged in my work and allows me the opportunity to make a living doing something that I love."

Tshibanda loves her new path and has found that not having a mentor is one of the few negatives she has encountered on the road to her success. She believes a mentor would help her develop comfort with her marketing strategy to take her business to the next level.

One disadvantage she feels has not unduly impacted her success is her race.

"Since being on my own, thankfully, I've not encountered a problem getting or retaining clients because of my color," says Tshibanda.

Tshibanda is an example of how a seemingly fatal set back in Corporate America can be the impetus for running out to take on your path with everything you've got.

"The company I worked for was sold and my department's function is now handled out of the new owner's corporate headquarters. I never knew what a blessing it could be to lose your job!" Tshibanda says. "I don't have a boss to report to. I don't have to deal with stupid office and corporate politics. Furthermore, I wouldn't trade the flexibility and lack of stress in my current path."

Tshibanda lives as an example of how obstacles can be blessings in disguise and how lack of coming from a rich family should not inhibit your aspirations.

- The key support you should start with after yourself is your family. Use good judgment in deciding how they can best support you.

- Good friends can be an emotional sail that help you handle the winds of change as you pursue your path.

Angels to support you on the path happen when you're looking and when you're not looking as long as you are clear on where you're going.

Chapter Ten

Measuring Success After You've Arrived At Your Destination

When I do good, I feel good; when I do bad,
I feel bad, and that is my religion.
—Abraham Lincoln

Signpost: Creating a new life for yourself for a path out of Corporate America can be a challenge and requires constant evaluation to make sure you stay on path.

Pat Yourself On the Back

Well, you did it! You got your butt off the proverbial couch and changed your life.

It's not a small thing to make a move away from Corporate America and it's a huge thing to leave it all together. Corporate America, if it's nothing else, can seem like a big old safety net. But sometimes that safety net seems stretched over an ocean or over traffic 40 floors below you.

Even at its most negative, working your job in Corporate America comes attached with familiarity and security. And with those things come comfort, and we all like to feel comfortable.

Walking a path outside of Corporate America will be invigorating, joyful, exciting, empowering but rarely comfortable.

As I write this, I've just received my first real royalty check from my first book, I've got training and consulting work scheduled for the next three months and a contract sitting in front of me that will make me part of a Washington, D.C.- based speakers bureau.

But am I comfortable? Far from it. Because with the exception of the royalty check which barely covers two months expenses—all of it is scheduled but not guaranteed income. If everything promised comes through as expected, I have enough money to get me through a long cold winter barring any emergencies.

But in the life of a person taking a departure from Corporate America, an emergency may be nothing more than not being able to work for a period of time because of illness, surgery or some circumstances beyond your control.

When you work for Corporate America you may not have the luxury of unlimited job security but you do have the luxury of having a regular paycheck to look forward to while you still have the job. And most traditional jobs include benefits and paid time off for vacation and sick leave.

So, how do you measure success? How do you determine whether this was the right move for you?

Actually, I think you measure it backwards. At the beginning of the analysis I suggested that you take a good long and hard look at your budget before deciding whether to leave Corporate America. I said that was particularly necessary if you had a spouse, life partner or dependent relatives, such as children, to consider.

Well, if you're already out and the question is whether you should stay out or go back, I think money is absolutely the last consideration you should rely on.

As sculptor Ed Hamilton says, "No one can lay me off and no one can fire me, so if I fail and don't follow through on a job, then it's my own fault and I have no one to blame but myself. For me, failure is not an option."

Making the Shift in Lifestyle

When you're in Corporate America you've already created a life-style for yourself that you've become adjusted to. Even if you just graduated from college last year and your brand new Toyota Civic is your only symbol of success, it's still a lifestyle you made for your-self by choice or maybe by automatic pilot. In your lifestyle of working steadily in Corporate America that's where you are and you've probably become very used to it.

Once you leave however, it's like taking the genie out of the bottle and trying to stuff her back in after she's tasted cheesy grits in Chicago and shaken her tail feathers on New Orleans' Bourbon Street—that bland little round cushion just won't be the same.

As Gary Johnson says, "My current path is better because I have control of my time that allows me the work/life balance that is so critical to success as I define it. Working for an organization does not allow me the freedom and flexibility to utilize all my talents. For example, BlackMenInAmerica.com would never have developed if I worked a corporate gig."

Intangible Benefits of Creating A New Life for Yourself

The benefits of entirely removing yourself from Corporate America to pursue your path create dozens of intangible benefits.

Therefore, to measure whether you are a "success" in your endeavor, you have to grab that same journal I recommended earlier and create a scale. From there, you place everything on the scale starting with feelings.

Feelings are important. Feelings determine your attitude, your stress levels, how you approach life, even your health. For example, one study has shown that people who have chronic anger or hostility in their life in their 20s are seven times more likely to be dead 25 years later as compared to their peers who didn't sweat the big stuff, the small stuff and everything in between. Other studies have linked excessive negative emotions to having a lower immunity system.

Sometimes, with the burden of racism never far from our conversations and thus, our minds, we sometimes don't stop to get in touch with what propels us forward.

Think back to how you felt on your typical days when you worked at your Corporate America job. How did your body feel? Tense, relaxed? Have you ever been diagnosed with health problems while working in Corporate America? Such as high blood pressure or any other stress related ailments?

If you were experiencing any health ailments or symptoms while working in Corporate America, have you noticed any relief or change in frequency since you left as a black traveler?

If you have experienced relief, then your health is better, at the very least your quality of life has improved.

On the other hand, if you had stress-related ailments while working in Corporate America that have gotten worse since you followed your path, you need to take a hard look at whether continuing on your path is in your best interest. But before you abandon your path, ask yourself what other things in your life also changed, such as relationships, family issues, money?

When I first quit my career as an attorney, I had a health problem with my reproductive organs that began to get better almost immediately. Stress aggravated the problem which caused pain. My close friends noticed in the first few months after quitting that I complained of pain much less.

However, fast forward a few months after that when the financial toll of making less money caught up with me. At that point, the ailments got so bad it caused more pain and more physical problems than it ever did, and surgery became required.

I briefly thought about returning to practicing law but the thought practically made me double over in pain. What I realized was the true problem was money—the need to spend less and make more. With that decision made and changes instituted to put it into place, I finally began to see the benefits of my decision. Right now Etta James pumps from my stereo singing "The Blues is My Business and Business is Good" while writing a book about something close to my heart. That wasn't going to happen if I went back to a law firm.

For me, I know that the stress I felt in Corporate America would have only worsened if I stayed. Sure, good money would have delayed that possibility, but not halted it.

Creating Newer, Happier Experiences for Yourself

A recent study has shown that more money and more possessions do not create happiness, but good experiences you can remember do. In fact, the article I read said that between using money to buy your family a big screen television and spending money on a memorable family vacation, go for the family vacation.

That gets back to whether continuing on your path as a black traveler is a success or not. Weigh your best experiences and see how they compare.

Compare if the benefits of Corporate America can be replicated in the life you've chosen on your path and vice versa.

For example, if you make a list of the three best things you liked about your workday in Corporate America, do you see how that is fulfilled in your life as a black traveler, and when you think of the three things you like best in your path as a traveler can they be replicated in Corporate America if you decide to go back?

The three best things I liked about my jobs in Corporate America (being a journalist and then later an attorney) were: the camaraderie of having co-workers, the status attached to my different jobs and having a certain routine to count on every week. The three things I like best about being a writer and consultant are: the fulfillment I feel from writing, the variety of the work I do and the control I have most of the time over my priorities and time.

As a writer and consultant I can creatively incorporate the best of Corporate America in my workdays: I make sure I call and/or email at least one friend in the morning during the days I work from home and schedule regular lunch dates with former colleagues who became friends; I still get to have the built in status carryover from my previous careers as well as my current one and I make sure that I schedule some routine into each day from the silly to the serious.

In terms of going back to Corporate America to work as a lawyer at any law firm or corporate office, it will be impossible for me to write anything more creative than legal memorandums which I hated doing: I will have limited control (say non-existent) over the variety of my work and no meaningful say over how I arrange my priorities and time.

And all those nice, linear issues aside, I just know that no matter how great the job starts I always end up feeling caught in a chokehold when working for a bad employer and end up feeling suffocated with a satin pillow when working for an essentially good employer.

In addition to processing your feelings and your health to balance whether leaving Corporate America was a good decision, you then must look at the health of your finances.

Even though I don't believe that money should be the first area you explore in determining success, it's admittedly a pretty high priority. When I talked about how the stress of my finances took its toll on me after quitting law, in was in large part because I was a single woman with no one else to rely on for income. If I don't bring in the bread, I'm toast.

Darrell L. Williams is a poet and musician who works as an assistant production manager at a small company and he knows how difficult it can be to make money while making music.

His life in somewhat traditional Corporate America included being a high school math teacher, a social worker and a professional soccer player for two years. Williams did all this after receiving a college degree in marketing.

It took him many years of figuring out what he wanted to do by eliminating what he didn't want to do.

"I held many jobs in various fields because I wasn't really sure what I really wanted to do as a career. Throughout the years, I've always kept writing poetry and playing bass guitar," Williams said. "Basically, I work to pay bills, and that's it. I don't aspire to be a career nine to fiver. I have aspirations of being a professional writer or musician, so I always keep my eye on goals while I work jobs that I can tolerate to pay the bills. I now believe I'm in a position where I enjoy my job, but it allows me the time to pursue my true dreams."

Williams has found that one of his largest obstacles in moving forward more quickly on his path is location, location, location as they say in real estate.

"I live in an area of society that appears to have the sole ambition of working, getting married and living in the suburbs. I don't want to fit into a comfortable middle class mold," says Williams. "Living in the Midwest stifles my ability to come in contact with people that share my love for music and poetry, and can help get me to where I want to be as far as being a writer/musician is concerned."

Williams, like that of most black travelers plunging forward on their path, finds that money is one of the key resources he needs to have more of.

"Unfortunately, I haven't had the finances nor the opportunity to move to a place that has an environment that would nurture my aspirations," Williams says. "I am the type of person that goes for my dreams and tries to reach high levels of achievement, no matter how low the chance of success. I am a free spirit and will try almost anything once. If all these musicians and writers listened to all those people who told them they would never make it, we wouldn't have such great music and words to experience."

Looking to Tomorrow to Decide If You're Happy With Today

When deciding whether to continue on your path you have to be willing to look at the long term financial implications of your change. You have to look at more than just the number in your bank account; you have to forecast where it will be in a year, in five years, in 10 years if you stay with your course of action.

You also have to ask yourself what financial sacrifices you will need to continue to make if you're making less money than you need. Are there lifestyle changes you have to make to stay on your path? Sell your house? Take in a roommate? Move to a cheaper place? Cash in your savings? Do moonlighting?

Because ultimately, success in any endeavor is based on figuring out just what you're willing to do to get what you want and what you're willing to give up if necessary. If you feel like you've given up everything you're willing to give up to embark on your path and you have nothing more to give, you do have to ask yourself it it's worth it.

In weighing whether you are a success in your new life you also have to look to see how this change has affected your family and personal life. Is your family happier because you're happier? Has any financial difficulty caused excessive harm? Have other life changes in the family been hurt by your change? It's almost impossible to consider yourself a success if your home life becomes a failure.

At the end of the day, what defines success is whether you've achieved your goals and objectives and done so joyfully. Without joy, without passion there's no point in creating a new path.

Anyone who has ever truly struck out on the path of the black traveler knows there is no going back even if emergencies force you to go back. The genie can go back in the bottle but the inside doesn't seem so spacious and comfy anymore.

This book was written to celebrate the black travelers who expanded their worlds to create a life worth living. I hope this book helps set in motion a new wave of black Americans who are able to forge new worlds and create new journeys. And I also hope it's a sufficient thank you and tribute to the black Americans who've been on these new paths for years.

I'd like to end this book with words of wisdom from a source that touches all lives, speaks to all hearts. In the words of the great Dr. Seuss, "Be who you are and say what you feel, because those who mind don't matter and those who matter don't mind."

Whatever path you end up taking or continue to take, don't forget to stop and enjoy the scenery along the way.

- Deciding to leave Corporate America—in whole or in part—is an act of courage that deserves a pat on the back.

- Making the shifts in lifestyle require constant reevaluation to make sure the path you've made for yourself keeps working for you.

- Part of determining success in your new life is figuring out whether you could replicate the same joy in your life if you returned to Corporate America.

- Making the new path for yourself is about enjoying the destination along the way.

If you have built castles in the air, your work need not be lost, that is where they should be. Now put the foundations under them.
—Henry David Thoreau

Resources

Books and websites to help with planning and goal setting

- *The Magic Lamp: Goal Setting for People Who Hate Setting Goals* by Keith Ellis

- *Wishcraft* by Barbara Sher

- *The 7 Habits of Highly Effective People: Powerful Lessons in Personal Change* by Steven Covey

- *Working From Home: Everything You Need to Know About Living And Working Under the Same Roof* by Paul and Sarah Edwards

- *What Color Is Your Parachute?* by Richard Nelson Bolles

- *How to Be an Entrepreneur and Keep Your Sanity : The African-American Handbook & Guide to Owning, Building and Maintaining Successfully Your Own Small Business* by Paula McCoy Pinderhughes

- *Your Money or Your Life: Transforming Your Relationship with Money and Achieving Financial Independence* by Joe Domingues and Vicki Robin

- *The Occupational Outlook Handbook* by the U. S. Department of Labor (revised every two years, the book describes what workers do by occupation, working conditions, training and education needed, earnings and expected job prospects)

Books and websites for those on the path of the Emperor

- *Success Runs in Our Race: The Complete Guide to Effective Networking in the Black Community* by George C. Fraser

- *Six-Week Start-Up: A Step-By-Step Program for Starting Your Business, Making Money, and Achieving Your Goals!* by Rhonda Abrams

- *Kick Start Your Dream Business: Getting It Started and Keeping You Going* by Romanus Wolter

- www.entrepreneur.com : Provides tips for starting own business and offers great guidance to other resources

- www.cdfi.org: This is a national network that includes information on community development loan funds, community development banks, community development credit unions, microenterprise lenders, community development corporations and community development venture capital funds. The CDFI Coalition coordinates industry wide initiatives to increase the availability of capital, credit and financial services to low-income communities across the nation.

- www.blackenterprise.com: Website from the magazine with a wealth of article and resources including a search engine for those looking for franchise opportunities

Books and websites for those on the path of the Artisan

- *How to Survive and Prosper as an Artist*, 5th ed.: *Selling Yourself Without Selling Your Soul* by Caroll Michels

- *187 Tips for Artists, How to Create a Successful Art Career—and Have Fun in the Process!* by Kathy Gulrich

- *Art Marketing 101: A Handbook for the Fine Artist* by Constance Smith

- *Black State of the Arts: A Guide to Developing a Successful Career as a Black Performing Artist* by Tanya Kersey-Henley and Bruce Hawkins

- www.artschool.com: A website for searching from among more than 3,500 art schools and programs around the world by area of specialty

- www.artjob.org: A website for those in the visual arts looking for professional opportunities and career information, including internships, fellowships and conferences.

- www.grants.gov: Website to find opportunities to gain grants for artistic projects

Books and websites for those on the path of the Hermit

- *Free Agent Nation: The Future of Working for Yourself* by Daniel H. Pink

- *A New Breed of Expertise: How Independent Consultants, Free Agents, and Interim Managers are Transforming the World of Work* by Marion McGovern

- *Free to Succeed: Designing the Life You Want in the New Free Agent Economy* by Barbara Bailey Reinhold

- www.monster.com: Offers advice and a free newsletter sent by email for contract and temporary workers to get advice on taxes and managing your temp career

- www.natss.org: The website of the American Staffing Association which allows you to search for jobs by state, skill set and job type

Books and website for those on the path of the Magician

- *What Should I Do With My Life?: The True Story of People Who Answered the Ultimate Question* by Po Bronson

- *Shine: A Powerful 4-Step Plan for Becoming a Star in Anything You Do* by Larry A. Thompson

- *Success Never Smelled So Sweet: How I Followed My Nose and Found My Passion* by Lisa Price and Hilary Beard

- *Having What Matters: The Black Woman's Guide to Creating the Life You Really Want* by Monique Greenwood

- www.mindtools.com: A website designed to help you think out of the box about designing your life, offers quizzes and articles, along with showing you how to find a life coach

About the Author

Michelle T. Johnson, Esq., a native of Kansas City, Kansas, has been working while black since the age of 14. One of her earliest jobs was at a library, where her interest in books flourished into a love of the written word. Michelle attended school in Kansas City, Missouri, and continued to feed her hunger for all things literary by working in libraries while in high school and in college at the University of Kansas.

While at KU, Michelle was bitten by the reporting bug and majored in newspaper journalism. She had summer internships at newspapers in Rochester, New York and Louisville, Kentucky. One of the highlights of her college experience was working as a columnist for the campus newspaper, which gave her the opportunity to interview Gordon Parks, a personal hero whose autobiography "Choice of Weapons" inspired her on her path.

Once she received her journalism degree in 1986, Michelle worked at the *Philadelphia Daily News* for a short stint before working the duration of her journalism career at the *Louisville Courier-Journal* and the *Austin American-Statesman*. Michelle was able to combine her concern for community and civic issues and her love of writing by covering the neighborhoods, and transportation beats at the *Louisville Courier-Journal*, and the drug and alcohol and county government beats at the *Austin American-Statesman*.

Upon deciding that the role of mere observer was not her strong suit, Michelle decided to pursue a career in law. Michelle attended the

University of Missouri-Columbia School of Law, where in 1994 she was named, by the Missouri Supreme Court, as the Top Moot Court Oralist of her law school. She received her juris doctorate in 1995. With a strong interest in employment law springing from both her personal experiences and those observed, she focused on the concentration of employment litigation.

Moving back to Kansas City, Missouri to be near her family, Michelle has worked the bulk of her years as an attorney in litigation law firms representing companies whose employees have brought complaints against them. To give herself a well-rounded experience in the field of employment law, Michelle opened her own law firm, and briefly worked as a solo practitioner, primarily representing employees who had complaints against their employers. During this time Michelle also worked as an administrative hearing officer for the city of Kansas City, Missouri, conducting hearings for citizens who have brought complaints regarding violation of the city human rights laws.

Currently, Michelle is a writer, public speaker, mediator, as well as a human resources and diversity consultant in Kansas City, Kansas, where she lives with her dogs Hilbert and Henry.

ORDER FORM

WWW.AMBERBOOKS.COM
African-American Self Help and Career Books

Fax Orders: 480-283-0991
Telephone Orders: 480-460-1660
Online Orders: E-mail: Amberbks@aol.com

Postal Orders: Send Checks & Money Orders to:
Amber Books Publishing
1334 E. Chandler Blvd., Suite 5-D67, Phoenix, AZ 85048

____ *The African-American Family's Guide to Tracing Our Roots* $14.95
____ *Literary Divas: The Top 100+ Most Admired African American Women in Literature* $16.95
____ *Beside Every Great Man...Is A Great Woman* $14.95
____ *How to Be an Entrepreneur and Keep Your Sanity* $14.95
____ *Real Estate and Wealth...Investing in the American Dream* $15.95
____ *The African-American Writer's Guide to Successful Self-Publishing* $14.95
____ *Fighting for Your Life: The African American Criminal Justice System Survival Guide* $14.95
____ *Urban Suicide: The Enemy We Choose Not to See* $14.95
____ *How to Get Rich When You Ain't Got Nothing* $14.95
____ *The African-American Job Seeker's Guide to Successful Employment* $14.95
____ *The African-American Teenagers Guide to Personal Growth, Health, Safety, Sex and Survival* $19.95
____ *No Mistakes: The African-American Teen Guide to Growing Up Strong* $14.95
____ *Black Out: The Black Person's Guide to Redefining A Career Path Outside of Corporate America* $15.95
____ *2007-2009 African American Scholarship Guide for Students and Parents* $15.95

Name:_____
Company Name:_____
Address:_____
City:_____State:_____Zip:_____
Telephone: (____) _____E-mail:_____

Tracing Our Roots	$14.95	❑ Check ❑ Money Order ❑ Cashiers Check
Literary Divas	$16.95	❑ Credit Card: ❑ MC ❑ Visa ❑ Amex ❑ Discover
Beside Every Great Man	$14.95	
How to be an Entrepreneur	$14.95	CC#_____
Real Estate and Wealth	$15.95	
Successful Self-Publishing	$14.95	Expiration Date:_____
Fighting for Your Life	$14.95	
Urban Suicide	$14.95	**Payable to:** Amber Books
How to Get Rich	$14.95	1334 E. Chandler Blvd., Suite 5-D67
Job Seeker's Guide	$14.95	Phoenix, AZ 85048
Teenagers Guide	$19.95	
No Mistakes	$14.95	**Shipping:** $5.00 per book. Allow 7 days for delivery.
Black Out	$15.95	**Sales Tax:** Add 7.05% to books shipped to AZ addresses.
Scholarship Guide	$15.95	**Total enclosed: $**_____